MW00915812

This book is dedicated to my dad, Allen Van Fossen. Thank you for teaching me so many of these skills. I love you and hope you're doing great up there in heaven.

Table of Contents

Note to the reader:

Thank you for buying my book. I hope you enjoy it, and I hope you find it useful and informative.

Trying to accurately predict the future movements of the financial markets is a fool's errand. It cannot be done. With this book I am in no way trying to predict what will happen to the financial markets in the future. Nor am I claiming that I can. Any references to past performance should not be taken as a prediction of future performance.

A quick point of disclosure—I am an Investment Advisor Representative registered in the state of North Carolina. As such, I do advise clients on how to best manage their finances, and for that service I receive compensation.

Personal finance is a complex area. I have done my best to give a perspective to these issues, calling out those where there is general consensus among financial professionals and those where there are starkly divided opinions. That said, given that predicting the future of financial markets accurately is impossible, that uncertainty will always breed different perspectives and opinions, even among those most knowledgeable in this field. I strongly encourage you to seek out a broad array of perspectives on these topics.

There is a significant amount of analysis using historic data. While I have done my best to ensure the calculations are accurate, they may not be. This may be due to mistakes I have made in my calculations, as well as approaches that I have taken which other knowledgeable financial professionals may disagree with. It is important that you do your own research and again seek out diverse perspectives on the calculations and perspectives offered here.

While I have done my best to convey perspectives based on the facts as I best understand them, again I may have made mistakes. This is true for everything in this book, but especially as it relates to specific laws and regulations. Regulations regarding personal finances are constantly in flux, as is the tax code of the United States and every other country in the world. This book represents my best understanding of these issues at the time of writing. However, those understandings may be inaccurate because I misunderstood them or because they have changed since this book was written. I strongly encourage you to gain those understandings for yourself, either on your own or by consulting a knowledgeable professional.

Finally, everyone is different. While I have tried to give perspectives that apply to a broad range of people and their situations, everyone's particular situation is unique. The best advice will not come from a book written by an author who has never met you and doesn't know your particular circumstances. Again, I encourage you to do you own research on what best applies to your situation and also to seek out professional advice from someone who can customize that advice to you.

PART 1: IN THEORY

This first part of the book is meant to offer a grounding in the theory, history, and philosophical approach to investing.

Chapter 1: *The Building Blocks of Personal Finance*

The first thing to do when learning about personal finance is to go over a couple terms, the first of which is the most basic: money. Money is one of those weird words, maybe similar to "food" or "life", that everyone knows what it means, but coming up with an actual definition isn't all that easy.

Such terms are difficult to define, especially at the edges. A hamburger is clearly food, and a rock is clearly not food, but what about chewing gum? A puppy is clearly alive while a gallon of water clearly is not, but what about an apple seed?

Similarly, we all know money is something we get usually for some type of work, and that we can then spend on things we want. Obviously, dollar bills are money but what about a small share of ownership in a company like Apple, or a promise from someone else to pay you for a share of Apple at some point in the future, or the option to buy a share of Apple at some specific price in the future? It can get complex very quickly.

Also, there is the distinction between money and an investment. When does something go from being money to being an investment? Can something be both at the same time?

Let's jump in.

Cash

The most basic type of money is cash. Physically, this is those coins and paper notes you have. Increasingly, cash has evolved away from the physical and now, especially in richer and more developed countries, exists as accounts on computers.

Either way, whether it's dollar bills (or euros or yen or yuan) in a person's pocket or numbers on a computer screen that shows the balance of their bank account, this type of money serves the same purpose. It is the primary medium that people use to get compensated for their work and then use to obtain the things they want.

In this basic way, cash is a facilitator of transactions needed for life. A person works and needs to be paid, so she is paid in cash. She takes that cash and uses it to buy things like food, shelter, clothes, and entertainment. It is not an investment (more on that in a second); rather it's a lubricant for life maybe the same way oil in a car's engine is. It allows life to work in a complex society with many different jobs people can do and with many different goods and services they can buy.

Investments

Before talking about types of investments like stocks or bonds or even cash, it's important to define the term.

An investment is something where a person gives someone else money (or something of value) with the expectation of getting that initial amount back plus some additional amount at some point in the future.

There are two universal elements of every investment: time and return.

- **Time**—An investment inherently involves some amount of time that the investor is without his money. He gives his money to someone else and sometime later, maybe days or weeks or years later, he gets it back. No matter how it's done, there has to be an element of time.
- **Return**—An investment also inherently involves a return after the time period is done. An investor needs to get back more than she gave, or at least enter the transaction with the expectation that she will get more back than she gave. If there is no return, such as a friendly loan between buddies or something like that, it can't be called an "investment".

Bonds

Bonds are probably the most obvious example of an investment that people think of. They are loans to some type of organization, most commonly a government or a company.

An investor will buy a bond issued from a government, let's say. The investor gives the government money and in return the government gives the investor a bond. At a high level, that bond is a promise to repay the investor. More specifically, the bond lays out the details of the repayment.

For example, Mary may choose to buy a bond. She purchases a US government bond for $1,000, and then the US government will promise to pay her back $1,100 twelve months from now, giving her a $100 return for her troubles. For bonds that return is usually called "interest," so Mary earned $100 in interest.

Both elements of an "investment" are fulfilled: Mary gives away her money for a year (time), and Mary does this with the expectation that she will get her initial amount back plus an additional $100 (return).

Interest payments are the main way that investors earn a return with bonds. However, there is a second way; investors can sell bonds before they mature. If investors sell a bond for more than they paid for it, that would also be considered part of the return. Of course, the converse is also true and investors could sell the bond at a loss, and that would diminish the return.

There are a ton of names for bonds that you may hear, but they all act in basically the same way—the investor gives someone money and gets back a specific amount sometime later.

- **Bills**—investments like Treasury Bills are loans that typically range in time from about 4 weeks to a year.
- **Notes**—investments like Treasury Notes are loans that typically range in time from about two to five years.
- **Bonds**—investments like Treasury Bonds or Corporate Bonds are loans that last for longer periods of time, about 20 to 30 years.

In this book the term bond will be used fairly interchangeably with all these types of debt investments.

Stocks

Stocks, along with bonds, are the other obvious example of an investment that people think of. That said, they act fundamentally differently from bonds.

Whereas a bond is a specific promise to repay a loan with interest at some point in the future, stocks are a slice of ownership in the company. One share of Amazon (at the time of this writing) costs about $150. There are a total of 10 billion shares of Amazon out there so, that single share is worth one-ten billionth of the company.

For example, Steve may choose to buy a share of Amazon at $150. He does so with the expectation that it's worth more than $150 over time. There's a lot of complexity here, much of which will be covered in subsequent chapters, but again, the criteria of an "investment" are met, albeit much murkier than in the example of a bond.

Whereas Mary's bond had a very well-defined time frame, twelve months, Steve's stock does not. Steve will own the stock forever, or at least until he chooses to sell it. Also, Mary's bond had a very well-defined return, $100, but for Steve it's totally unknown; maybe Amazon stock will be worth twice as much as he paid for it in the future or half as much or any other value.

Another major difference between bonds and stocks is there are no government stocks. For bonds all sorts of entities can issue debt: companies, governments, individuals, etc. That is strictly not the case for stocks; only publicly traded companies can issue stock. While a person could invest in Amazon bonds (with the promise of a specific interest rate and specific time of repayment) or in Amazon stock (with an expectation that the stock increases over time), that is not the case with governments.

Government bonds are extremely similar to corporate bonds. But there is no such thing as government stock. Buying that single share of Amazon stock gives an investor a small sliver of ownership of Amazon Corporation. The US government is not an entity which is owned by individuals so there is no such thing as stock in the United States.

Some stocks pay their shareholders periodically. These payments are called dividends. They can be thought of as the company giving a portion of its profits back to the shareholders. Dividends are commonly paid on a quarterly basis, so in this way they are very analogous to the interest payments for bonds. Similarly, dividends are part of an investor's return.

Also, similarly to bonds, stocks can be sold at more or less than they were bought for. This profit or loss also counts towards the stock's return to the investor.

In this book the term stocks and "equities" will be used interchangeably for these types of investments.

Stocks and bonds are the most important investment categories there are. Also, for typical investors, these two are the only investments a person should have. That said, the investing universe is incredibly complex with many other categories out there. Here are a few of the most common investment categories after stocks and bonds.

Derivatives

Derivatives are a broad term for a class of investments that are based on the value of simpler investments, most commonly stocks or bonds. There are innumerable flavors of derivatives like options, futures, and swaps, and more coming out every day.

Most derivatives, aren't commonly used by individual investors. Rather the majority are used by companies and financial institutions. That said, one common form of compensation for people, especially as they get higher in the corporate ranks, is stock options. So, it is important to mention them here and their role in a person's investment portfolio will be discussed in future chapters.

An **Option** is an investment where an investor has the option but not the obligation to purchase an asset. This is an important feature that introduces a lot of complexity.

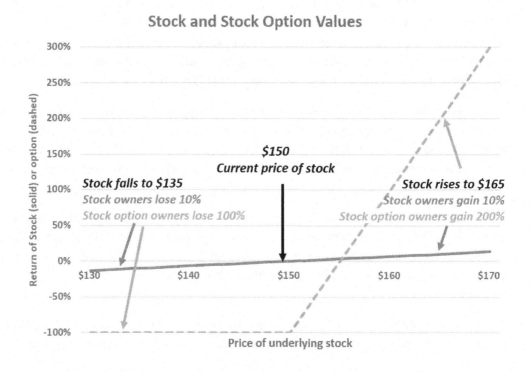

For example, Maria may purchase an option to buy a share of Amazon stock, which is currently trading at $150. Maria would pay $5 (the pricing of options is extremely complex, but for the purposes of this example, just assume the option costs $5) for that option. She would have one year to "exercise" her option, after which it would expire and become worthless.

If the stock doesn't do well, either stays at $150 or even falls below $150, Maria would choose to not exercise her option and walk away from the transaction. She would have paid $5 for the option and would lose that money, but beyond that she wouldn't have any other loses due to the fall in Amazon's price. On the other hand, if the price of Amazon rose she would have the ability to buy the stock at $150. If Amazon did really well and rose to $165, she would have the option to buy it at $150, realizing an immediate $15 profit. After subtracting the $5 she paid for that option, her net profit would be $10.

A really important feature of derivatives, and one that makes them unsuitable for most investors, is that they are extremely leveraged. Small movements in the value of the underlying asset (a share of Amazon) can lead to huge changes in value of the option. If Amazon's stock fell or even stayed the same after one year (a fairly common occurrence), the value of the option would be worthless, a 100% investment loss (yikes!!!). Conversely, a small increase for Amazon's stock, maybe 10% or going from $150 to $165 (a similarly common occurrence) would result in a 200% return for the option.

The nearby table shows how the value of both a share of stock and a stock option can change. Both the stock and the option are dependent upon the value of Amazon stock in this example. As Amazon stock goes up, so does the value of the stock itself by definition (the solid line). If Amazon goes from $150 to $135, the value of Amazon stock would fall $15, or 10%; conversely, if Amazon rose from $150 to $165 then the value of the stock would rise 10%. That all is pretty simple.

Stock options become more complex. In our example with Maria, she paid $5 for the option to buy Amazon stock at $150. If Amazon stock stays at $150 or falls, Maria's option becomes worthless, and her return is -100%. When Amazon fell from $150 to $135, the stock decreased 10% in value, but the option decreased 100%!!! On the other hand, if Amazon rises from $150 to $165, Maria's option gives her the right to buy that share for $150 even though it's really worth $165. She makes a gross profit of $15 ($165-$150). Since she paid $5 for that option, her net profit is $10. That's a huge gain. The shareholder would gain 10% when the stock moved to $165, but the option holder gained 200% (a $10 profit on a $5 investment).

It becomes very clear that losses become worse with options, and wins become better with options.

Commodities

Commodities are investments in things like oil or gold or corn. An investor buys the asset (although rarely takes physical possession of it). The goal for investing in commodities is similar to that of stocks: buy something now with the expectation that its value increases in the future.

However, there is a major difference between investing in commodities and stocks. For stocks, the investor is giving the company money, and the company is supposed to do something with that money that creates value. It could be developing a new product that consumers will want, building a new factory to produce stuff faster or cheaper, expand into a new market, and on and on. A government may build a bridge or an airport. Whatever it is, the idea is that the investment is being used to create something that is better than what exists currently. Whatever it is, the company or the government is trying to create new value, making the pie bigger, so to speak.

With commodities, the investor is buying something and then holding it until it becomes more valuable. The oil the investor buys sits in a storage tank doing nothing until it's sold. The oil isn't creating value by powering some machine; it's just waiting until someone else wants to buy it. In this way, it's a zero-sum game. The investment is profitable only to the degree someone is willing to pay more than the investor did. No value is being created; the pie is staying the same size.

Because of this, commodities are a very different type of investment compared to bonds or stocks, and investors should have very different expectations for the types of returns commodities should provide.

Mutual funds

Mutual funds have become the dominant investing vehicle for most investors. Yet, mutual funds aren't really an investment class themselves as much as a way to invest in the categories mentioned above.

A mutual fund company will create a portfolio of many different assets and then sell shares of that asset pool to investors. For example, Vanguard may buy $100 million of shares from all the companies that compose the S&P 500. Here Vanguard may make each mutual fund share worth one-one millionth of the total portfolio, so each share is worth $100. An investor could buy that mutual fund share for $100.

Over time if the value of those S&P 500 companies goes up, the value of Vanguard's portfolio goes up, and therefore the value of that mutual fund share the investor bought goes up. Mutual funds have a huge advantage in that they allow regular investors to buy a largely diversified (much more on the concept of diversification in later chapters) portfolio for a small amount of money.

In this example, the investor owns a small piece of each of the companies in the S&P 500 for the low price of $100. Without a mutual fund, the investor would need to buy 500 individual stocks which would cost tens of thousands of dollars. Plus there would be the huge headache of actually going online to place all those trades. It wouldn't be practical. A mutual fund allows investors to do that with tremendous ease. Because of this, mutual funds are really the only type of investment most people should make.

Mutual funds can be composed of any investment type. We just used the example of a mutual fund made up of stocks from the S&P 500, but a mutual fund could be composed of any types of stocks—technology stocks, Asian stocks, high-dividend stocks. It can also be for bonds. There are mutual funds composed of different types of bonds. Some mutual funds have a mix of all types of bonds while others focus on government bonds or only short-term government bonds or short-term corporate bonds. There are mutual funds that are a mix of stocks and bonds.

The range of mutual funds is limitless. Truly, there is probably a mutual fund out there for any mix of stocks and bonds that can be imagined. For the purposes of this book, we'll refer to mutual funds that are totally composed of stocks as **equity mutual funds**, those composed totally of bonds as **bond mutual funds**, and those composed of a mix of stocks and bonds as **balanced mutual funds**.

Annuities

Another type of investment is annuities. Annuities give investors monthly cash payments for the rest of their lives.

An investor could take $100,000 and give it to an annuity company, and then that company would pay the person $200 each month until the person dies. That monthly amount would be mostly based on the person's age; the older the person, the higher the monthly payment would be.

That monthly payment from an annuity looks very similar to the monthly payments of a bond. However, while a bond as an end date when it is fully paid off and the payments stop, annuity payments go on until the person dies. Due to these similarities, it's common to think of annuities very similarly to bonds.

While it is possible for people to buy annuities as described above, they are most common either as a work benefit or a government benefit. Some companies offer their retired employees an annuity. In the United States, the Social Security program offers citizens an annuity in their older years.

Indexes

Indexes are not an investment per se, but rather a measuring stick by which investments are assessed. Imagine the question: "Did stocks go up or down over the last year?"

Clearly, it's an important question. Investors certainly want to know how things are going in the investment world. However, it isn't necessarily an easy question to answer.

There are thousands of stocks out there. Over any period of time, some will be up and some will be down. Some of those that are up will be up a lot, while others will barely be up; same thing for those that are down. But such an answer would not be very helpful.

The solution is an index. An index is a weighted average of many stocks. The most famous index is the Dow Jones Industrial Average. It takes the prices of 30 large US stocks, and averages their performance. When the Dow is up 2%, that means overall those 30 stocks are up on average 2%, even though individually some may be up more than 2% and others less.

Just like there are countless mutual funds out there, there are countless indexes. They each measure the stock market a bit differently. The S&P 500 measures the 500 largest US companies. The Russell 2000 measures smaller US companies. The FTSE measures British stocks and the Nikkei measures Japanese stocks.

All these indexes are used by investors to have a simple, quick way to measure the overall movement of the stock market.

In later chapters indexes will again show themselves as the basis for creating mutual funds. In fact, index mutual funds (where the components of a mutual fund are selected to mimic an index) have become the dominant investing tool for most investors.

Chapter 2: *Historical Perspective*

The whole point of investing is to make a return. That begs the question: "What return will I get on my investments?"

The simple answer to that question is, "No one knows." By its nature the stock market is unpredictable. There is deep research as to why the stock market behaves as it does and what makes it so unpredictable, especially in the short term. We will cover some of those concepts later, but suffice it to say for now that the future movements of the stock market, especially over the short-term, are impossible to accurately predict.

That said, we can look to the past to get a sense of how the stock market does behave, how that varies as an investor's time horizon changes, and how that varies for different asset classes like stocks or bonds.

Historic data sources

Fortunately for investors, there is no shortage of data. It gives us a trifecta: it goes back for a really long time, there is detailed data on nearly everything you could imagine, and it is fairly easy and inexpensive to obtain and analyze.

Extremely detailed data for nearly every American stock (unless otherwise noted, when I refer to stocks, I will be looking at US stocks) and bond ever traded goes back to the 1930s in the CRSP database. Monthly data for the stock market as a whole—inflation, interest rates, and dividends—goes back to 1871 with Nobel Prize winner Robert Schiller's data. Daily price data going back to the 1950s can easily be accessed on Yahoo! Finance.

This treasure trove of data can be sliced and diced a million different ways to get a perspective on how stocks and bonds have performed in the past. It's a really important point to understand that historic performance doesn't guarantee future performance, but this can give us insights as to what could happen.

Stock performance

Since 1871 stocks have had an average dividend rate of about 4%. On top of that, the prices of stocks have increased about 6%. If you add those up, you get an average return for stocks of about 10%.

But the term *average* is really, really important. In 1931 the stock market had its worst year ever, down 43%; and then a couple years later in 1934 stocks had their best year ever, up 55%. Those were right around the Great Depression which was a crazy time for the stock market, but there are similarly crazy numbers today. In 1995 the stock market was up 35%, and then in 2008 it was down 35%.

Mathematically the statement is true that on average the stock market has returned a total of 10%, but there are major swings. As an investor, it's critical to consider both the return as well as the volatility.

Time is on your side

Another critical feature of stock returns is that while they are extremely volatile over the short term, they are much less volatile over the longer-term. In fact, this concept is apparent in the nearby table.

	Average return	Worst year	Best year
1871-1880	9%	-14% (1877)	48% (1879)
1880-1900	6%	-19% (1893)	29% (1889)
1900-1920	9%	-24% (1907)	38% (1908)
1920-1940	11%	-43% (1931)	55% (1933)
1940-1960	15%	-12% (1946)	46% (1954)
1960-1980	8%	-21% (1974)	39% (1975)
1980-2000	18%	-7% (1981)	35% (1995)
2000-2020	8%	-35% (2008)	32% (2009)

Stock returns from year to year can vary wildly, ranging nearly 100% from the worst year to the best. Yet, looking at a longer time horizon (in the table it is 20 years) the returns vary 12% from the period with the lowest returns to the highest (6% in the 1880-1900 time period and 18% in the 1980-2000 time period). Statistically, it's called reversion to the mean; in investing lore it's called patience.

Using the same data set we can look at stock returns for varying lengths of time. For this analysis let's assume a person invests $10 every month for 12 months. At the end of those 12 months, the person will have invested a total of $120. If the person started in January 1871 and ended in December 1871 that $120 would be worth $128 because of the overall rise in the stock market over that period of time.

If you look at every 12-month period from 1871 to 2022 (there are about 1800 of them), that investor would have made money 73% of the time.

We can do that same "monthly investment" analysis for differing lengths of time, from as short as a single month to thirty years. This gives us a very important result.

	% Profitable	Average annualized return	Worst return	Best return
1 month	63%	12%	< -90%	> 100%
2 months	64%	12%	< -90%	> 100%
3 months	66%	12%	-89%	> 100%
6 months	69%	12%	-76%	> 100%
1 year	73%	12%	-71%	> 100%
2 years	78%	11%	-62%	53%
5 years	88%	10%	-42%	37%
10 years	97%	9%	-14%	27%
20 years	99.9%	9%	-0.4%	18%
30 years	100%	9%	2%	16%

* Returns are annualized.

There are three key insights here. First, the longer the time horizon for investing, the more likely it has been to be profitable. If an investor just looks at investing for a single month, he would have made money 63% of the time. Conversely, he would have lost money 37% of the time.

However, there is an obvious trend. The longer the investment time horizon the more likely an investor has made money. To the point that since 1871, there has not been a single instance where consistently investing over 30 years would have lost money. There has only been one instance where consistently investing over 20 years would have lost money; that was starting in June 1912 and having the terrible luck to be in the depths of the Great Depression 20 years later.

Of course, it is impossible to predict the future of the stock market, but using history as a guide, steady investing over 20 years almost certainly results in a profit.

The second key insight is that no matter the time period, the average return stays the same, roughly within a narrow range of 9% to 12%. This is important in that the stock market always has an *expectation* that it will go up over any given time period, be that a day, a week, a month, a year, or a decade. Reality can be very different from that expectation, but over the history of the stock market, that consistent pace is reflected over different time horizons.

The third insight is that volatility greatly decreases with a longer time horizon. The spread between the best and worst years swings wildly. For a single year, the spread is from -71% to over 100%; that is an enormous range. But, in an extremely consistent manner, the longer the time horizon, the smaller the spread. At 30 years it has narrowed from 2% to 16%, a mere 14% range.

This relationship between time and investment volatility will have profound implications for investing strategy.

Bond performance

A similar analysis can be done for bonds, or any financial asset really, and it would display the same trends. Bond prices vary over time, and the longer the time period, the less likely they have been to lose money. Also, over longer periods of time, the range of the variance of bond returns tightens, just as it did with stocks.

That said, bonds do behave differently from stocks. Namely, the returns of bonds have been lower, and the volatility of those returns from year to year have also been lower.

Bond returns can be analyzed, both short-term bonds and long-term bonds, going back to the mid-2000s (the returns for bonds are a bit harder to come by compared to stocks). Comparing the average returns along with the best and the worst years for bonds alongside stocks we see two obvious trends.

Returns from 2006 to 2023	Average return	Worst Return	Best return
Stocks	9%	-37%	32%
Long-term bonds	5%	-27%	22%
Intermediate-term bonds	4%	-12%	10%
Short-term bonds	2%	-5%	7%

First, bond returns tend to be less than stocks, with short-term bonds offering a return less than intermediate-term bonds which in turn off a return less than long-term bonds. Second, the volatility of bond returns is less than that of stocks, with again short-term bond volatility being less than that for long-term bonds. The near-by table illustrates this, looking back to the time period from 2006 to 2023 for stocks (VFINX), long-term bonds (VBLLX), intermediate-term bonds (VBILX), and short-term bonds (VBIRX).

Lower returns are associated with lower volatility. This will be an important relationship which will similarly have profound implications for investing strategy.

Chapter 3: *Risk and Reward*

Imagine the perfect investment. It would have high returns, like a stock. It would also have steady returns, like a savings account. And with this perfect investment, your monthly account statement would be delivered to you by a unicorn galloping down a rainbow.

Sadly, as is the case with unicorns, such an investment is fantasy. However, it does illustrate the fundamental tradeoff of personal finance—high returns versus steady returns. This yin and yang sits at the very core of investing, and it will drive nearly every decision an investor makes.

There is an enormous swath of financial products out there that offer investors a wide spectrum of options. They range from those with low risk and low reward to high risk and high reward.

Lowest risk, lowest return

The least risky investment, perhaps it can be thought of as the "safest" investment a person can make is with cash in a **savings account**. That money would be 100% guaranteed by the FDIC, so it would be impossible to lose money. Also, the return would be very predictable. An investor would know with a high degree of certainty how much he would get in a month or a year from his savings account investment. Finally, it would be extremely accessible. The investor could take the money whenever he wanted, in a day, a week, a month, a year or ten years.

Unfortunately, all this convenience and safety comes at the cost of very low returns. Savings accounts have among the lowest returns of any asset class.

Another term that is often used for this type of investment is **money markets**. Savings accounts tend to be held with banks, while money market accounts act nearly identically but are typically held in brokerage accounts.

Certificates of deposit (CDs) are similar to savings accounts, offering a bit higher return. They are similarly safe, also insured by the FDIC. However, when an investor buys a CD she commits to investing her money for a specified period of time, anywhere from a couple months to a couple years. Whereas a person can withdraw her money from a savings account any time she wants, that's not the case for a CD. It is that decreased accessibility that requires CDs to offer a higher interest rate. If they didn't offer that better rate, people would always just use a savings account and never a CD.

For the purposes of this book, I will refer to these types of investments as "cash". Returns for these investments vary with changes in interest rates, but a good general rule of thumb for returns on cash is about 1%.

Medium risk, medium return

A step up the risk spectrum are **bonds**. Bonds are associated with two types of risk. First, there is "repayment risk". This is when the bond's value doesn't get repaid. Perhaps the company who issued the bonds fails and isn't able to repay the loans. Maybe the government's debts overwhelm its finances and it declares bankruptcy. The United States has never defaulted on its debt but other countries have like Russia (1998 and 2022), Argentina (2014, 2020), and Turkey (1982); within the United States some municipalities have defaulted like Orange County, California (1994).

The second type of risk with bonds is "interest rate risk". There is a whole chapter dedicated to this idea, but for now know that a bond's value is affected by the prevailing interest rates in the market. If overall interest rates increase the value of a bond falls, and if interest rates decrease the bond's value goes up.

Compared to cash, both these types of bond risks make them less safe: they are more likely to result in an investment loss, and they are less accessible. For all these reasons, bonds offer higher returns than cash.

Of course, all bonds aren't created equal. Some bonds are riskier. Corporate bonds tend to be seen as riskier than government bonds, so the corporate bonds usually offer higher returns. Debt from third-world countries have higher default rates than first world countries, so those bonds need to offer higher returns.

From the perspective of a bond's maturity (the length of time until the bond is fully repaid), long-term bonds will drop in value more when interest rates rise than will short-term bonds. Predictably, the general rule is the longer a bond's maturity, the higher the return.

Certainly, bond returns vary widely, but a good estimate is about 4%.

Highest risk, highest return

The riskiest asset class is **stocks**. They are the riskiest because of their "residual value" nature. Imagine a company that issues both bonds and stock. Bonds have a higher priority than stocks, so they are always paid off first. If there isn't enough money to pay off the bonds *in full*, by definition there isn't *anything* to pay the stock holders.

In this way stocks tend to be more "feast or famine". In the good times the bonds are paid off and then all the extra profit goes to the stockholders. However, in the bad times, all the money goes to the bondholders and the stockholders get little or nothing.

Similar to bonds, there are different types of stocks that generate different returns, always of course based on the perceived risk of the company.

Larger companies tend to have more predictable earnings than smaller companies, making their stocks less risky; hence, large-cap stocks tend to have lower returns than small-cap stocks. Similarly, stocks from emerging markets are perceived as riskier so investors expect higher returns. Equities can be categorized in a million different ways and the common theme always emerges: the higher the expected risk of the company, the higher the expected returns.

Historically, as was outlined earlier, returns on stock vary wildly, so any ideas of an "average return for stocks" needs to be taken within that context. However, most people assume a return of 8-10%.

The nearby table shows the average return and volatility of different types of investments. Looking at the period from 2006 to 2023, it shows the average return as well as the highest and lowest annual returns for short-term bonds (VBIRX), intermediate-term bonds (VBILX), long-term bonds (VBLLX), large-cap stocks (VFINX), and small-cap stocks (VSMAX).

The clear trend shows that the less risky an investment (short-term bonds), the lower the average return and the smallest range from best to worst, a proxy for the "safety" of the investment. At the opposite end of the spectrum, the riskiest investments are small-cap stocks which have near the highest average return and the largest range between their best and worst years.

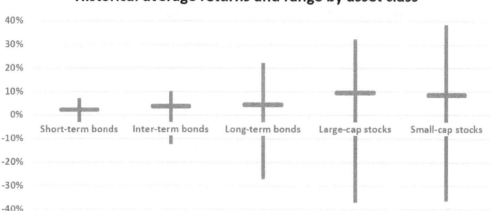

Historical average returns and range by asset class

Higher returns with lower risk (if only)

It's human nature to take life as it is, and wish it was better. That is certainly the case here.

If only there was a way to have the safety and predictability of cash or bonds but with the returns of stocks. Sadly, there isn't. There's no good way to increase those returns of those "safer" investments

However, the converse does have those possibilities. With stocks there is a way to keep those high returns while reducing the investments risk. This crazy alchemy is called time.

History shows that stocks return on average about 10% each year. But any single year has tremendous uncertainty. 30% of the time stocks will lose money when looking at a one-year time horizon. The range for annual stock returns here is a 170% swing from best to worst. That is crazy volatility, and stock holders are compensated for taking it on with the higher returns.

Yet, the data also clearly show that over longer time horizons, the volatility decreases dramatically. That 30% chance of stocks losing money in any given year goes down nearly to 0% if you look at the time horizon in terms of decades. That 170% range shrinks 15% with that generation-long outlook.

From a statistical perspective, stocks do become less volatile over longer periods of time, all the while average returns remain the same. To the degree an investor thinks of less volatile investments as less risky, he's getting his cake and eating it too. He can get the higher returns associated with stocks with less risk. He just needs to be committed to the investment for decades. While that may seem like a long time, when thinking of retirement planning, it really isn't.

Historical annual stock returns based on time-horizon

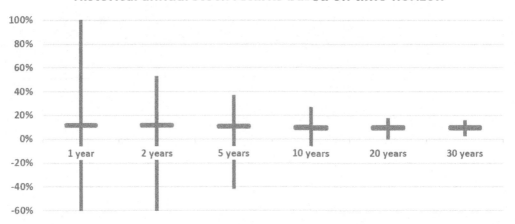

That's not to say that risk is eliminated. Even over long periods of time, there are still ups and downs. That will never go away.

This concept, that stocks become less volatile over the long-term is a critical element of financial planning.

Chapter 4: *Diversification*

One of the most important concepts in personal finance and investing is diversification. Actually, this tends to be sage wisdom for life with idioms like *don't put all your eggs in one basket*. While that may apply broadly in life, it's especially important here. Yet for all its importance, it is commonly misunderstood and misapplied.

The simple definition for diversification is picking different investments from the same investment class in order to reduce the risk of the portfolio. From previous chapters we know that risk and return are inextricably linked in investing. Higher returns come with higher volatility. Diversification acts as a magical elixir, allowing an investor to keep her returns high while reducing her volatility.

Reducing risk with diversification

Let's use Terry as an example. He decides it is appropriate for his $100,000 net worth to be invested $80,000 in stocks (how he came up with that weighting of stocks is a question of Asset Allocation which will be covered in a later chapter). Now Terry needs to determine *which* stocks to invest in.

There are thousands out there. Also, Terry is a strong adherent of the Random Walk theory (more on this investing theory in a later chapter), so he knows even if he just picked a stock randomly it has just as good a chance as any other stock of doing well or poorly. Based on all that, what should Terry do?

The short answer is Terry should invest in a mutual fund that mimics the overall stock market by investing in a small sliver of every company out there. Now let's determine why that's the right answer.

Looking at the two extremes, Terry could pick one single stock and invest all his money in that, or he could invest in that mutual fund which is really taking his money and splitting among hundreds of different stocks. Mathematically, the return Terry should expect from either strategy is the same. The expected return from a single stock is the same as the expected return from the entire stock market.

The real difference comes in the risk Terry is taking on when he invests in just a single stock. Here, risk will be defined as how volatile the returns are from year to year. Terry would prefer an investment with lower risk (i.e., steadier returns) compared to one with huge swings up and down, assuming the overall returns are equal.

This idea is best illustrated with a real-life example. From 1984 to 2023, the S&P 500 went from about 165 to about 4770. When you include dividends that's an astonishing 14% average annual return. It was a really good time to be an investor over those 30 years with the computer and internet revolutions.

From 1984 to 2023	S&P 500	ADM
Average return	14%	14%
Best year	38% (1995)	75% (1989)
Worst year	-37% (2008)	-37% (2008)
Years above 20%	14	16
Years below 0%	7	13

Instead of the highly diversified portfolio of the S&P 500, let's say Terry randomly picked a single stock from the 500 that make up that index. As stated previously, a single stock should have the same expected return as the whole index, so let's magically pick a stock that had about the same return over those 30 years as the S&P 500 (in reality, about half the stocks would do better and about half would do worse).

The stock that fits that criterion is Archers-Daniels-Midland (ticker symbol ADM), an agricultural company based in Chicago. Just like the S&P 500, over those 30 years ADM had an average return of 14%. From a raw return perspective, Terry should be indifferent between investing in ADM or the S&P 500.

This is where volatility comes in. ADM was much, much more volatile than the S&P 500, even though they both had the same overall return. ADM's best year was a

75% return which is double the best year of the S&P 500, but ADM offset that by many more bad years. In those 30 years, the S&P 500 had a negative return in 7 years, while ADM went negative 13 times.

An investor wants high returns but that's just one side of the coin. The investor also wants lower volatility. In this case the return was the same but ADM had more extreme ups and downs.

The moral of the story is diversification gives those same high returns but reduces the volatility, as was the case with the S&P 500. Having multiple stocks allows them to offset each other. When one stock is down the other might be up, and vice versa. From an investing theory perspective, that lower volatility coupled with an equal return makes an investment like the S&P 500 clearly superior to ADM alone.

What to pick

Mutual funds, by their very nature, are really good at giving investors diversification. That is actually their primary purpose.

In a world of thousands of mutual fund options, which should an investor pick? The concept of diversification wants to cast as wide a net as possible. The S&P 500 is very diversified among large, US-based companies, but it lacks diversification among mid- and small-cap companies; it also lacks diversification among international companies.

The financial services industry is extremely good at identifying needs and meeting them, so it's no surprise that the gaps for a mutual fund composed of stocks from the S&P 500 have been filled. Vanguard offers a mutual fund which offers total diversification across all sizes of companies and all regions of the world—Vanguard's Total World Index Fund (VTWAX). Fidelity doesn't have a single fund that does all that, but it does have a total fund for the US (FZROX) and one for international (FZILX) which combined provides total diversification.

Beyond stocks, there are broad mutual funds that offer total diversification for bonds, for commodities, and foreign currencies.

That said, some people ask if it's necessary to diversify within mutual funds: *If you have one total US market mutual fund (Vanguard's VTSAX), does it make sense to diversify with another total US market mutual fund (Fidelity's FZROX)?*

The answer here is no. Within a sector, mutual funds typically have total overlap so the diversification doesn't do anything. Certainly, between different sectors (let's say US and World equities), there is value in diversifying, but not within the same sector.

Chapter 5: *Fees and Expenses*

Like every other industry in a capitalistic society, the financial services industry charges its customers for the goods and the services it provides.

These fees come in a diverse array. There are mutual fund management fees that mutual funds charge investors to recoup the costs of running their funds. There are transaction fees that brokerages charge investors to buy and sell securities. There are advisor fees that investment advisors charge to give advice to clients on what to do with their portfolio.

Opinions on these fees vary as widely as the fees themselves. Yet, the stakes couldn't be higher. Compared to the more "typical" expenses we have in life like groceries or vacations or accountants, fees charged to investors tend to be higher, more confusing, and less connected to real value. For those reasons, these warrant a deep dive.

Major impact on net worth

Fees can have a major impact on an investor's net worth. Everything a person buys—car payments, health insurance premiums, tickets to the opera—all cost money and by definition they all reduce a person's net worth. Yet, investing fees seem to have a more profound impact than other things.

Let's take Barry. He invests $10,000 each year in his 401k. With an 10% return, after 40 years the math says that Barry should have about $4.4 million.

However, Barry uses a financial advisor who charges him 1% of his net worth to manage his finances. Also, Barry's advisor puts him in mutual funds that charge an annual management fee of 0.5%. In total Barry is paying 1.5% in fees annually.

After taking into account those fees, value of Barry's account falls from $4.4 million to about $3.0 million. That's a huge impact, around $1.4 million. Compared to what it would have been without fees, Barry's net worth was reduced by about one-third. That is a profound impact.

Swept under the rug

One of the reasons financial fees are so insidious is that they seem insignificant, leading most people to ignore them. Yet the Barry example clearly shows how huge their impact can be.

Most fees in the industry are quoted in percentage terms. Most financial advisors charge their fee as a percentage of assets under management. Fees vary, but usually are around 1%, plus or minus. Mutual funds, which as mentioned earlier should be the primary investment vehicle for most people, charge fees to run their mutual funds. These fees vary widely, ranging from 0.0% to as high as 1.5% or even more.

Brokerage fees are charged when an investor buys or sells stocks or bonds. These also vary widely with some offering this service for free, while others charge as high as $20 per trade.

The common theme is that none of those numbers seem all that large, yet their impact is huge. One or two percent seems insignificant. It's the extra sales tax the county puts on top of the state sales tax that you don't even notice. It's the transaction fee you're charged when you buy tickets to a concert. It is annoying but it's only a couple bucks so not really worth getting upset over.

Yet, that small percentage when multiplied by a really large number like the thousands or millions of dollars in your investing portfolio becomes a very large number in itself. When those fees are charged year after year, it really adds up.

In the example of Barry, towards the end, as his portfolio grew to the million-dollar range, he was paying close to $10,000 annually. Normal expenses at that level would typically draw a lot of scrutiny. Most people are well aware of the amount of their car payment, and most people understand that paying more would give them a nicer car and also that they could lower their payment by getting a car that isn't as nice.

There are a million other examples of major expenses (on the scale of $10,000 annually or about $1,000 monthly) that people scrutinize. However, for some reason (likely that the fees are quoted in percentage terms), financial fees get a pass. But those fees add up to have an enormous impact on an investor's net worth.

Mutual fund management fees

One of the reasons that financial fees are so galling is there is no clear evidence that a person is getting value for the money he is spending. With most things people pay money for, there is a clear connection between the "goodness" of what it bought and how much is paid for it.

A nicer car costs more than a crappier car. A really good meal at a nice restaurant with a cute atmosphere cost more than a meal at a fast-food place. A knowledgeable personal trainer will cost more than a doofus. In almost everything people buy, they are good at discerning quality and value in their purchases, but this profoundly breaks down when it comes to financial fees.

Mutual fund fees are the best (or should they be called the "worst"?) example of this. Nearly every investor has mutual funds, and all mutual funds charge management fees. On the surface, there is nothing wrong with charging these fees, per se. Mutual fund companies provide an extremely important service—they allow normal investors the ability to simply and easily invest in a broad, diversified portfolio of stocks or bonds with a single investment. Compared to what someone would have to do without mutual funds—buy hundreds or thousands of individuals stocks or bonds—that's an incredibly valuable service.

Very justifiably, mutual fund companies should charge for that service. Also, they incur costs in providing that service; there are expenses for filing with the SEC and other regulatory agencies, there are marketing expenses there are IT expenses to keep the fund running and allowing people to see the value of their investments. The list goes on and on. Those are legitimate expenses, and there is nothing wrong with mutual fund companies charging investors for that.

However, things start to look a bit ugly when one digs a little deeper. There is a huge range of mutual fund management fees as was mentioned above—from literally 0% to above 1.5%. What is an investor getting when he pays 1.5% that he wouldn't get when he pays 0% (and the example of Barry shows how large that 1.5% fee can add up to)? Certainly, if mutual funds that charged a higher fee had better returns, that could be worth it.

This very point has been researched extensively in academia. As it turns out, there isn't any meaningful link between management fees and performance. Study after study has shown that mutual funds that charge lower fees do just as well as mutual funds that charge higher fees. It's an uncomfortable fact, and one that a multi-billion-dollar industry has a huge motivation to subterfuge. Nonetheless, the data consistently show in study after study that there just isn't a lot of value here.

Financial advisor fees

Another big expense in the financial industry are financial planner fees. There are a ton of people who advise investors and charge a fee for that service (full disclosure—the author is an Investment Advisor Representative from the state of North Carolina).

Similar to mutual fund management fees, investment advisor fees can range widely. 1% of total assets under management is a good rule of thumb for this, although some charge higher levels (the state of North Carolina lists anything higher than 2% as "high fees" and anything above 3% as "excessively high") while others charge less.

As with mutual fund management fees and every other thing that people buy, there should be the question: *Is the amount the financial advisor is charging worth it?*

Here the data is much more mixed. Everything a financial advisor does can be done by an individual investor free of charge. Certainly, financial advisors bring knowledge and know-how, but even that is fairly easy to come by for an investor (such as by reading this book). An individual who takes a few dozen hours to educate herself on this could easily do 98% of what an investment advisor does, all the while saving that fee.

A person *could* do that, but does a person actually do that? This is where investment advisors show their legitimate value. For people who don't want to think about their investments and don't want to take the time to learn the skills, outsourcing that to an investment advisor can be worth it.

The data here is much harder to come by than the analysis on mutual fund fees, so it's worth a jaundiced eye. However, a few studies do show working with an investment advisor increases an investor's returns by more than the advisor charges.

The most famous study is one commissioned by Vanguard (which is ironic since Vanguard pioneered low-cost investing and working directly with consumers). This study showed that investors who work with an advisor have returns about 3% higher than those who don't. After subtracting the advisors fee (use 1%), that means the investor gets a 2% higher return. That is a significant number that can lead to a lot of money over an investing lifetime.

The study broke down where that 3% came from. Some of it was know-how—the advisor picking more appropriate funds based on the investor's situation (asset allocation) or funds with lower management fees. Some of it was also emotional steadiness; investors with advisors were less likely to make shortsighted decisions during market turmoil like cashing out after a market crash. There is certainly value there, so from that perspective investment advisors may be worth it. However, all those things the study showed advisors do to create value are very simple things that investors can do on their own; so maybe there isn't value there after all.

Freefall of fees

For all the negative aspects surrounding fees and expenses, it is worth noting that today investors have it better than they ever have. Fees have fallen to incredibly low levels. Compared to the average investor as recently as the 1990s, fees charged today are unimaginably low.

A generation ago (think of the 1990s as "way back when"), transaction fees were much higher than they are today. If an investor wanted to buy shares of a company, $100 per trade was a common fee. If she wanted to trade an odd lot, less than 100 shares, it might cost more.

Imagine Christine was an investor then. She has a portfolio of $100,000, and she has that spread over 12 different stocks. She makes 12 trades a year, once per month, which seems reasonable. That's $100 to sell shares and then another $100 to buy the new stock she wants. In a given year, she'll spend $2,400 on trading fees. That comes to 2.4% of her portfolio.

Today, the brokerage firms with the higher fees tend to charge about $20 per trade. Fees of $100 are absolutely unheard of. Even better, many large companies like Vanguard and Fidelity offer investors $0 trades. That's a huge windfall for someone like Christine.

Over that same time period, mutual fund management fees have plummeted. Back then there was an orgy of fees: a fee for the initial investment, a fee for early redemption, an annual management fee, and on and on. Today most of those are gone and those that remain are much lower than they were.

Imagine Dillion was an investor back then. He has a $100,000 portfolio and he invests it in a mutual fund. First, there were things called "loads". This was a fee on the initial investment, and these tended to be huge, in the 5% range. For just investing with the mutual fund, Dillion paid $5,000. Then each year Dillion would pay a mutual fund management fee; these fees were higher than now, and 1% was probably an average level. So that was another $1,000ish per year. His first year he's paying 6% in fees which is crazy. In subsequent years he's paying 1% which is still very high.

Today, index mutual funds are the dominant investing vehicle (much more on index mutual funds in a later chapter) for ordinary investors. Loads are a thing of the past, so that's a huge savings. More importantly, mutual fund management fees have cratered.

In the 1990s index mutual funds charged about 0.25%. At the time that seemed microscopic compared to the 1% or more than actively managed mutual funds were charging. Over time that 0.25% has fallen to nearly zero; Vanguard's major index mutual funds have fees in the 0.05% range, and Fidelity has a line of mutual funds with 0.0% fees. Literally that entire fee has evaporated.

Chapter 6: *Interest Rates*

There are a million things that can make stocks and bonds go up and down. Fundamentally, the most important driver is the health of the company (or the solvency of the government in the case of government bonds).

If a company does well, namely generating and growing profits, the value of both its bonds and stocks tend to go up. The bonds will be less likely to default which increases their value. Since the stocks represent the overall value of the company, they will go up too.

That said, there is another factor outside the company's control which has a huge impact on the prices of stocks and bonds: interest rates. And the most important interest rate in the world is the US Federal Reserve Funds Rate. In fact, there probably isn't a single other event that can drive markets up or down as sharply as changes to the Fed's rate.

The federal funds rate

In the United States the Federal Reserve is an incredibly powerful and enormously complex organization. While it defies an easy description, it can be thought of as part regulator, part national bank.

It has a dual mandate: to maintain full employment and to promote price stability. In simpler terms its job is to help steer the country's economy along a healthy course.

Economic downturns like the Great Depression of the 1930s, Stagflation of the 1970s, and the Great Recession of 2008 are examples of when its employment mandate failed. Indeed those periods are considered the seminal failures of the Fed.

Similarly, periods of high inflation like in the early 1980s and more recently in the post-pandemic 2020s are the most recent examples of failed Fed policy with regard to price stability.

The primary tool the Fed uses to achieve this dual mandate is called the Federal Funds Rate. This is the rate that the Fed sets which banks charge each other for loans. When this rate is set, it trickles down to all other interest rates in the economy. If the Fed increases this rate, soon all other interest rates—mortgage rates, bond rates, CD rates—all tend to go up. When the Fed decreases the rate, all those other rates similarly fall.

Fed rate's impact on bonds

Changes to the Fed rate has the most immediate impact on bonds, since they are a direct instrument of interest rates.

The point is probably best illustrated with an example. Suppose Allen buys a bond for $1,000. It is a 10-year bond that pays 5% interest. When Allen buys the bond, the overall interest rate is 5%. That parity between the prevailing interest rate (5%) and the bond's coupon rate (5%) means the bond sells for its face value ($1,000).

Then the Fed raises interest rates to 6% (although in real life, the Fed almost never moves interest rates 1%; usually the moves are up or down 0.25%). All of a sudden, bonds start paying 6%. What happens to the value of the bond Allen just bought? His only gets paid 5%, so it's not nearly as valuable as the $1,000 bonds offering 6% interest. Allen's 5% bond decreases in value, perhaps to $950.

The opposite is also true. If the Fed lowers rates to 4%, Allen's 5% bond looks a lot more attractive. This will drive the price up from $1,000 to maybe $1,050.

The time horizon of the bond also plays an important factor. In Allen's example, he had a 10-year bond paying 5%. When interest rates went up his bond became less valuable, namely because he was stuck with a bond paying a lower interest rate for the next 10 years. Now imagine that instead of a 10-year bond at 5%, he had a 20-year bond at 5%. The rise in interest rates still makes that 5% look bad, but now he's stuck with that for 20 years instead of just 10. The rise in interest rates would hurt the 20-

year bond more than the 10-year bond, maybe making it fall down to $900, whereas the 10-year bond only fell to $950.

As a general rule, as interest rates go up, bond prices fall; and as interest rates go down bond prices rise. And those movements are correlated to the length of the bond. The longer a bond's time horizon, the more it moves up or down; shorter length bonds will still rise and fall counter to interest rates, but just not as much.

Fed rate's impact on stocks

The Fed rate has the same impact on stocks as on bonds—increasing the rate tends to lower stock prices and reducing the rate tends to raise them—but the mechanics of why this happens are much more nuanced.

An analogy often used is that of a car. The US economy is the car, the Fed is the driver, lowering rates is the gas pedal, and raising rates is the brake pedal.

The Fed can "accelerate the economy" (a commonly used term) by lowering rates. This allows companies and governments to borrow money more cheaply.

Cheaper money helps companies' profits, and therefore its stock price, in two ways. First and most obviously, it reduces the interest rate paid on debt.

Second and more importantly, it makes new projects or initiatives more profitable than they would otherwise be. Imagine a company has run the numbers and it knows that it could profitably expand its factory if interest rates are below 5%. So long as interest rates stay above 5% it doesn't expand, maintaining its current profits. However, if the Fed lowers the rate below 5%, the company then expands, making more profits associated with that expansion.

That's just one company, now imagine that across the whole economy with the thousands of companies. As the interest rate goes down, all of a sudden there become a lot more opportunities for profit compared to when it was higher.

The opposite is true too. The Fed can "pump the brakes on the economy" (another commonly used term) by increasing interest rates.

Why does the Fed do this?

It's undeniable that the Fed rate is an incredibly powerful tool that impacts the financial markets so profoundly. But why does it choose to accelerate or slow down the economy? This goes back to the Feds dual mandate—full employment and price stability.

Full employment means there are lots of jobs out there for people to have. Those jobs are created when interest rates are lower and companies can profitably take on new projects. In this way, lowering interest rates drives the economy towards full employment (or lower interest rates reduces unemployment).

On the surface that seems like an unambiguously good thing. Who wouldn't want a faster growing economy creating more jobs and more profits? But this is where too much of a good thing can become a bad thing.

If the economy is growing too quickly because companies have too many new projects and there are too many job openings, that can lead to inflation. Inflation is the general rise of prices, and it often arises from economies that are running too hot.

With so many job openings people will likely get higher wages. Companies with openings will need to pay more to attract workers. Current employers will have to pay their workers more to keep them.

Similarly, supplies like lumber or oil or computer chips or office space or all the million other things that companies need more of when they expand will see their demands increase. If there is only so much copper to go around and now there are new projects that need copper in addition to all the old projects that were using copper, the price of copper will go up. Apply that same logic to everything.

Wages and other costs will go up. Companies will raise their prices to offset this, and there will be a general rise in prices. This is the definition of inflation. While a small amount of inflation is viewed as healthy for an economy (and even this point is sharply debated), it is universally agreed that high inflation is bad.

These two competing forces become the balance that the Fed is trying to maintain. It needs to keep interest rates low enough that companies have jobs for the people, but not so low that the companies don't grow too fast in order to avoid inflation. It's a delicate needle to thread.

Chapter 7: *Taxes*

Pretty much anywhere money is involved, taxes are too. Personal finance is no different. In fact, taxes are probably the dominant driver in the accounts most people use to invest their money.

Quick note—The US tax code is enormously complex and constantly changing. The concepts discussed here are based on the author's understanding of the current tax laws. Additionally, everyone's tax situation is different so the concepts discussed here are meant to be applicable to the more common situations.

Income taxes and capital gains taxes

There are a ton of different types taxes: property taxes, payroll taxes, sales tax, inheritance tax, and many more. When it comes to investing and personal finance, the two most important are: income taxes and capital gains taxes.

As the name implies, income taxes are taxes on the income a person earns. This "income" can take many forms (and the IRS is eager to make this definition as broad as possible). Obvious examples are the salaries people earn, but that also extends to a salesman's commission, a waitress's tips, a retailers profit of what they sell something for compared to what they pay for it, and on and on. Any money a person gets from their work or labor is used for income taxes.

Capital gains are thought of and treated very differently. These are taxes on the profit a person makes from selling an investment. Generally speaking, if a person buys a stock for $50 and later sells it for $75, that resulting gain of $25 is taxed as a capital gain.

The nearby table which shows the taxes rates for a married couple in 2023, illustrating these differences. Both taxes are progressive, meaning that the rate at which a person is taxed is based on her income, and that tax rate increases as her income increases.

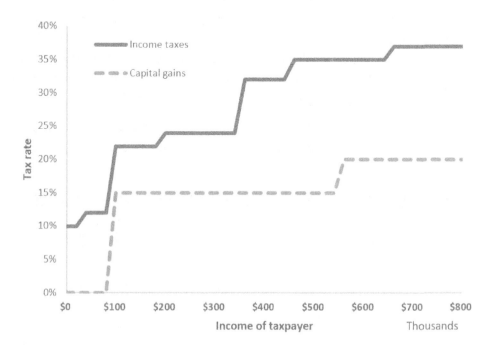

Income taxes are at a higher rate compared to capital gains taxes, and there are many more tax brackets for income tax (seven) compared to capital gains tax (three). The lowest income tax bracket is 10%, for married couples making less than $23,200; for capital gains taxes the rate is 0% until a couple's total income exceeds $89,250.

Tax-advantaged treatment for investments

Of course, taxes are a very important element for life overall in that they consume an extremely large amount of a family's income, probably the single largest line item, usually exceeding rent/mortgage and savings for retirement.

What makes taxes of particular interest to investors is how they are treated when different types of investing accounts are used. Most people have probably heard of the terms 401k, 403b, 529, IRA, or Roth IRA. These are all the types of accounts that investors can use to save money, and these all have been blessed by Congress to receive special tax treatment.

If someone were to save money in a regular account at a bank, he would get taxed coming and going. When he earned the money he used to fund the account it would be taxed as income. Then any interest or dividends he received would also be taxed.

Similarly, if someone opened up a brokerage account to invest in stocks or bonds or mutual funds, the same thing would apply. The money she put into the account would be taxed as income. Then while she held the investment, any dividends she earned would be taxed. Finally, when she sold the investment at a gain (hopefully it's a profit, which is the whole point of investing after all), the profit she made would be taxed as a capital gain.

That's a lot of taxes every step of the way. However, Congress in an effort to incentivize people to save for their future or college, has made special accounts that avoid some of those taxes along the way.

Pay taxes now and later	Pay taxes later, but not now	Pay taxes now, but not later
• Brokerage account • Savings account	• Traditional IRA • 401k	• Roth IRA • Roth 401k • 529

Pay taxes now, but not later

With a Roth 401k, Roth IRA, or 529 accounts, an investor pays taxes the year he contributes the money to the account, but then never again.

For example, Roger uses a Roth IRA to save money. He makes $100,000 annually and puts $5,000 into his Roth. Here, he is paying taxes on all $100,000 of his income, including the money he is saving in his Roth. So far there is no tax advantage with the Roth. Roger needs to be patient.

When it comes time to start withdrawing the money, Roger won't be taxed on any of it. All the interest and dividends that Roger earned in his Roth will be tax free. All the profits on his mutual funds which would normally be taxed as capital gains are all tax free.

Doing some quick, back-of-the-envelope math, it's easy to see the huge tax advantage for Roger. If he has a Roth IRA that he contributes to for his whole working life, let's say 40 years, he'll contribute a total of $200,000 ($5,000 each year for 40 years). He will be taxed on all $200,000.

When it comes time for Roger to retire and take that money out (401k and IRA accounts typically can't be accessed until age 59 ½) there is a huge pot of tax-advantaged gold waiting for him. Use some basic assumptions like his equity mutual funds increase 8% each year, and on top of that he gets a 2% dividend (10% total annually). Over those 40 years he will have contributed $200,000, and it will have grown to about $2.2 million. That's $2 million in profit, and he won't be taxed on any of it. That's a huge benefit, and that's the power of a Roth IRA.

Pay taxes later, but not now

The inverse of the Roth example is the 401k example. With a 401k or a Traditional IRA (for the rest of this chapter I will be referring to Traditional IRAs and 401k's interchangeably just because of their tax treatment), the person avoids taxes the year they contribute the money to the account (instead of paying taxes in that year, as is the case with a Roth), but then they owe the taxes when they finally withdraw the money in retirement.

A 401k is the most common type of account that most Americans have access to in order to save for their retirement. Just by virtue of this, it makes understanding this concept extremely important.

The mechanics work where a person saves money in a retirement account through their employer. The key feature which makes these accounts attractive is that all the money the person puts into the 401k does not show up on their tax statement as taxable income.

For example, assume Amy makes $100,000 per year. Normally, she would be taxed on all $100,000. However, if she contributes 5% of her income into her 401k, she saves $5,000, and that $5,000 is not counted as her income for tax purposes. So instead of being taxed on $100,000, she will just be taxed on $95,000. It's easy to see that would result in significant tax savings.

Traditional IRAs are similar, however while a 401k is done through a person's employer, a person can do an IRA on her own. With an IRA, whatever she contributes is tax deductible. So if she contributed $5,000 to her IRA, she would deduct that $5,000 from her income taxes. In either case, using a 401k or an IRA allows a person to reduce their taxes now.

However, there is a catch. Over time, those investments will increase in value. When the money is actually taken out, taxes on all the money will be owed.

This begs the question: Why do this if an investor still has to pay taxes, instead of now just later? That is where the progressive tax structure comes into place.

If taxes were flat and a person paid the same rate, no matter what, then there would be no advantage to a 401k or IRA. However, we know that when your income is higher, your tax rate is higher.

Now, think about the income of someone when she is saving for retirement in her 401k or IRA, and compare that to her income when she is retired and withdrawing those funds. Almost certainly, her income (and hence her tax rate) is higher when she's working and saving, compared to when she is retired.

Use Amy again as an example. At $100,000 (let's assume she's single just to keep things simple), her marginal tax rate is 22%. If she can reduce her income by $5,000, that is $5,000 less she will be taxed at 22%; that gives her a tax savings of $1,100.

Then she gets old, retires, and starts withdrawing from her 401k. Let's assume she lives on $40,000 annually. Because she is withdrawing so much less money in retirement compared to when she was working, her average tax rate will be about 10%.

And that, ladies and gentlemen, is the punchline; that is what makes 401k and IRA accounts worth it. Amy avoided paying taxes at 22% during her working years in order to pay taxes at 10% when she was retired. In the one year when she saved $5,000, the total tax benefit would be about $600 (12% of $5,000). Doing that year after year would result in significant tax savings.

Which is better, a Roth or Traditional IRA?

These two paths, the pay now/not later as with Roths, or the pay later/not now of a Traditional IRA, both have obvious and immense tax advantages. Given that most investors will have a choice between a Traditional 401k or a Roth 401k and between a Traditional IRA or a Roth IRA, it begs the question: *Which is better?*

As with every question ever asked in personal finance, the answer is: *It depends on your personal situation.* However, there are some basic assumptions that apply to most people which can give a more concrete answer.

In a world where tax rates don't change over time and where tax rates don't change with your income, there is no mathematical difference between a Traditional and a Roth. If one did the math, using the exact same contributions, the exact same investments, and the exact same returns; and only changed the tax impact of a Traditional versus a Roth, the final number would come out the same for both.

However, that world doesn't exist. The first variable is how tax rates will change over time. In a world where tax rates rise in the future, Roths are better. The taxes are being paid now rather than in the future when the tax rates will be higher. The opposite makes the case for Traditional IRAs; if tax rates are expected to fall in the future, Traditionals are better.

It's near impossible to predict what future Congresses will do with taxes, so here it seems most prudent to just assume that today's tax rates serve as an unbiased indicator of where future rates will be. So here, there's no clear advantage for a Roth or a Traditional.

The other, much more durable feature of the tax code is the progressive nature of tax rates. Tax rates are higher as income increases. It's been that way for over a century and there's no real reason to assume that will ever change.

This gives an undeniable advantage to a Traditional IRA/401k over a Roth. As the math showed with Amy, her tax rate is higher when she is working and making the most money. When she retires her income falls precipitously, and along with that so does her tax rate. In a flat tax rate world, the Traditional IRA and the Roth IRA would have identical results, but this tips the scale towards Traditional being better because the taxes are paid in retirement when taxes are lower, rather than while working when taxes are higher.

The catch with tax advantaged-accounts

There is no such thing as a free lunch, and that is the case here. This chapter started with the idea of a savings or a brokerage account being taxed coming and going—the money put into the account is taxed and then the gains on the investments are taxed.

These tax-advantaged accounts avoid much of those taxes which is what makes them so attractive, but there is a catch. The government created these accounts as tools of social engineering to drive behavior they wanted. Traditional IRAs, 401k's, and Roth IRAs are all meant to be savings vehicles to help people put money away for their retirement. 529s are meant to help save for educational expenses.

As such, these accounts have much less flexibility than does that simple savings or brokerage account. With those, you could invest as much as you want without caps, and you could withdraw as much as you wanted whenever you wanted. That is not the case with these tax-advantaged accounts.

The retirement accounts like a Roth or Traditional IRA or a 401k cannot be withdrawn until the investor turns 59 ½. Withdrawing the money early invokes sizeable penalties. Similarly, the education accounts like a 529 can only be used for qualified educational expenses; spending them on other things would incur similar penalties.

There is clearly a trade-off, and every person needs to decide for herself if the tax advantages offset the restrictions. For most people, this is an easy answer: "Yes, the tax advantages are definitely worth it."

For most people, the bigger question isn't *Should I invest with a tax-advantaged account?*, but rather *Should I invest in a 401k or a Roth 401k?* That answer could be worth tens of thousands of dollars.

Chapter 8: *Efficient Markets*

Early on in a person's investing career, there comes the decision of which investments he should make, and the idea comes in that says: *Let's just pick the stocks or the bonds that will do the best.*

Ahhhh, if only life were that easy. The stock market has thousands of individual stocks to choose from. Just pick the stocks that will do well and avoid the ones that do poorly. The idea is absurd, but it does prompt a worthwhile question as to *Why is it absurd?*

The seminal book on this topic is *A Random Walk Down Wall Street* by Burton Malkiel. It was first published in 1973 and several revised editions have come out over the years. On a personal level, I read this book in 1997 while I was in college when I was developing my thoughts on investing. It had a profound impact on my thinking on the topic, and I still think about those ideas and concepts to this day. I strongly recommend it.

A Random Walk

Rigorous academic research and practical application has shown that it is impossible to accurately predict the movements of the stock and bond markets. This applies in general, but particularly so with any level of precision and over the short term.

Rather, prices of stocks (for the rest of this chapter, I will refer to stocks but this more-or-less equally applies to bonds as well) follow a "random walk" pattern. That is to say, on any given day they could go up or down, it could be by a lot or not that much. No one really knows.

As long as there have been stocks there have been theories and strategies on how to select stocks to get the best performance. Pick high-dividend stocks or stocks that have fallen right after a bad earnings call or stocks with a high P/E ratio or stocks with a low P/E ratio or a thousand other strategies. The fact is, none of those strategies consistently and reliably deliver superior returns.

In the early part of the 1900s, the search for this holy grail showed promise. There were so many theories and so much data (the stock market has more data than probably any other aspect of humanity). However, there was no way to analyze that data to glean those insights that would reveal the stock picking strategy that wouldn't miss.

In the 1950s and 1960s as computers emerged, one of the first killer apps for that new analytic power was the stock market. All sorts of factors about stocks were analyzed and the results came back a bit surprising to the investing community—there's no real way to do better than the overall stock market. Hindsight is always 20/20, but there was no strategy that, if applied with the information available at the time, could lead to superior investing returns going forward.

Rather stocks just follow this random walk (so named after the staggering, meandering walk of a drunk person). There was no predictability. Randomly picking a stock was just as good a strategy as spending dozens of hours analyzing a company. That insight has profound implications for investing.

A God-send for regular investors

In a very real way, this is the best news possible for normal investors. It makes a level playing field for everyone. All of us—from the smartest and those who spend the most time thinking about stocks, to the dumbest and who don't spend any time thinking about stocks—all have the same chance of picking a winner.

This stands in contrast to other money-making endeavors. With sports betting a seasoned handicapper with years of experience could probably more consistently identify which thoroughbreds will win a race compared to a noob who bets on the horse with the coolest sounding name. In real estate, there are probably a ton of advantages to knowing the trends of the markets for different neighborhoods and the experience to know what sells and what won't.

But for stocks we're all created equal. That is very liberating. In some ways, this leads to unintentional comedy. Back in the 1980s, when this idea of a Random Walk was much less accepted than it was today, it was common for newspapers to pit a seasoned stockbroker's picks against a kid's, or a dartboard, or even a chimpanzee's. Hilarity would ensue when a few months would pass and the results would show those high-priced brokers would underperform as often as they would outperform. It was fun to hear a stockbroker humbled when admitting: "Bobo picking ABC stock was a real stroke of genius." As it is, your picks for the stock market are just as likely to do well as anyone else's, and that's a great thing.

Buyers and sellers in a market

The data clears shows that the stock market does follow a random walk, so it is important to understand *Why it does follow a random walk?*

The concept of the market place is what forces the idea of a random walk to work. By definition, a marketplace is where buyers and sellers come together to make transactions that are acceptable to both. Historically, it has been a physical place like Wall Street; today it is more of a concept facilitated by computers, networks, and the internet. Be it physical or virtual, the concept applies equally.

The key idea is that a buyer and seller must both agree to do the transaction. Let's use the example of a share of Amazon stock. If the stock trades at $150, that means the buyer was willing to give up $150 for the share of Amazon stock and the seller was willing to give up the share for $150.

If you assume that all investors, both buyers and sellers, are greedy (in finance academia they use the nicer term "profit motivated") then the buyer would want to buy the share for as little as possible, and the seller would want to sell the share for as much as possible. The buyer is willing to pay up to $150 but would love to only have to pay $50. Unfortunately, the seller isn't willing to go as low as $50. Similarly, the seller is willing to sell for $150 but would love to get $250. The transaction will occur only where there is overlap between the buyer and the seller. In this case that's at $150.

Now the random walk comes in. If today the consensus of buyers and sellers agree that $150 is the fair price for Amazon stock, that is where the trades will happen. However, if everyone knew that tomorrow some event would occur that would increase the value of Amazon stock to $160, then that is where the price will go *today*. Buyers would happily pay $150 today knowing tomorrow it would be worth $160, but no sellers would. In this way, if a stock is worth $X tomorrow, that is what it is worth today.

If there was a trading strategy that worked perfectly well that predicted today that Amazon stock would rise to $160 tomorrow, that is what it would trade at today. Therefore, the current price reflects all the information available today.

How this impacts investment choices

This idea drives most of our investment choices. The idea of trying to pick individual stocks is off the table. That means a broadly diversified mutual fund is almost certainly an investor's best bet. So much time and energy are saved just by this one concept.

Now investors can focus on the things that do matter and that can drive performance such as:

- **Asset allocation**—*How much of my portfolio should be in cash versus bonds versus stocks?* Once an investor decides on those weights, it's really easy to decide *which* stocks or which bonds to pick.
- **Time horizon**—*How does the timing for when I'll need the money impact my decisions?* There is a huge difference in appropriate investment choice depending on if an investor needs to have access to the money within a year versus in retirement 30 years from now. The good news is, as was discussed in an earlier chapter, this is a fairly easy concept to implement. The sooner the money is needed the less risky the investments should be.
- **Tax benefit**—*Which tax-advantaged accounts should I use?* This was discussed at length in an earlier chapter.

Some readers may identify a contradiction which is worth addressing. An early chapter noted that based on history, stocks do reliably increase over time. How can this be true while the unpredictability implied by the Random Walk theory is also true?

These can coexist because of a long-term time horizon and precision. First, the Random Walk theory looks at things in the short-term. It's impossible to know if stocks will rise or fall on any specific day. However, as the time horizon is expanded from days to decades, the randomness decreases and there is a clear upward trend in stock market prices which is undeniable. There aren't credible market participants who could dispute this.

Second, the Random Walk theory says stock movements can't be predicted with any precision, and that is absolutely true, even over the long-term. No one can say if stocks will go up or down tomorrow, and they certainly can't say if they will go up or down 4% or 10% or something else. It's just a guess. Even over the very long term, 30 years, the data shows that stocks return on average 9%, but there's still a range from 2% to 16%. Over the next 30 years it's pretty safe to predict that stocks will go up, but predicting how much they will go up is still a guess.

PART 2: IN PRACTICE

This second part of the book is meant to offer practical approaches on how to implement the concepts of the first part of the book into a successful overall investing strategy. As always, every individual is different so while this is meant to offer broadly applicable advice, it may not be appropriate for your particular circumstances.

Chapter 9: *Head Versus Heart*

One of the greatest challenges of investing is that people are humans, and humans evolved emotionally and intellectually in a manner that runs very contrary to what classical investing theory says is best.

This is often couched in a battle of your head versus your heart. Your head knows what the math and the data say. Your heart knows what feels right and makes you comfortable. When they are at odds, it's hard for you to pick the "right" choice, to the degree there even is a right choice. Typically, the head is the way to make more money.

In investing there's the famous idiom that "you can eat well or sleep well, but rarely can you do both." This is just the battle of our head (eating well) and our heart (sleeping well). And it doesn't mean we should always listen to our heads and not our hearts. If an investing strategy will maximize net worth but is so risky that the you can't sleep at night, maybe maximizing net worth isn't worth it. That's an individual call but it's very valid.

Psychological research has found most humans have what is called "loss aversion". Translating that to investing parlance, an investor would be more upset by a $100 investing loss than he would be happy by a $100 investing gain. This extends to an interesting insight. If those two events (the investing loss and the investing gain) are combined, the investor would end up where he started, no loss and no gain, but would feel worse (since the loss upset him more than the gain made him happy) than if he hadn't done anything. Both outcomes have the identical end result, no loss or gain, but going up and down (or down and up) made him feel worse. This oddity of human psyche has profound implications for how people feel about investing.

Another queer psychological characteristic of humans is we are really bad at finding the middle ground or being patient, two qualities especially important in investing. Investing theory prescribes not getting too excited when the market is on a tear, and not panicking when the market crashes. Yet investors often do the opposite— we pile in when the market hits new highs and we pull our money out when it plumbs to lows. This is the exact opposite of what we should do.

This quality likely traces back to early human evolution where there wasn't a lot of value in half measures. If the wandering tribe of cavemen found a really fertile grove of fruit trees or a stream teeming with fish, the clear choice was to stay there as long as possible and get as much food as they could. There was no concept of "maybe we should pace things out here".

Similarly, if a pack of saber-tooth tigers slaughtered half of the cavemen, the survivors didn't think about waiting it out to see if things improved. Rather, they got the heck out of there and fast. Humans evolved to survive in a very black and white world, and there was very little room to think about the gray. Yet investing is all about the shades of gray, and that is why so many people struggle with it.

Investing a windfall

This is a first-world problem for sure, but many of us at one point or another will get a large amount of money all at once. Maybe it's an insurance payout, a tax refund in April, a bonus check, or a bunch of cash that has accumulated in the checking account.

If you want to invest this money in the stock market, this becomes a head versus heart question of how to do that. Should you invest it all at once in one fell swoop or should you spread it out over several weeks?

The case for the heart goes back to that concept of risk aversion. If all the money was invested at once, many people would be totally freaked out that they would buy at the wrong time—either the day after stocks went up 1% or the day before stocks dropped 1%. Using a simple scenario of $10,000 to invest, that would mean you could "lose" $100 by investing at the wrong time. Of course, there is an equal probability that your timing could be great, investing right before the stock market went up 1% and "gaining" $100. Yet psychologically, people tend to dislike losing money more than the like making it, so many people don't like taking on that risk.

The alternative is to spread things out. Instead of investing the windfall all at once, and risking the timing being bad, you could invest a little bit over time. That would limit any major losses, but it would also limit any major gains.

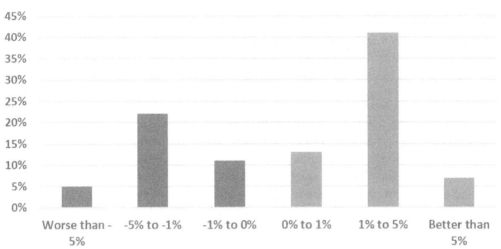

Advantage of one large investment compared to 10 investments spread over 10 weeks

Looking back at data from the S&P 500 since 1950, you can compare two different approaches:

1. Invest your entire chunk of money all at once
2. Spread your investment evenly, investing 10% of it each week for 10 weeks (dollar cost averaging)

The data shows that the first option, investing your money all at once, is the clearly better choice. It comes out on top about 61% of the time. On average, the first option has a 0.7% higher return. That's a lot of money.

The thinking is that historically, stocks have always gone up. Sure there have been some rough patches, some of which can last a really long time, but the general trend is definitely upwards. Waiting to invest your money over a longer time period has you missing out on some of that upward trend.

Yet so many people would prefer the second option because it feels safer. It is nice to have high returns, but you also have to sleep at night. Would that 0.7% higher return be worth your stomach being tied in knots? That's the choice of listening to our head versus our heart.

Owning company stock

A common question investors have is: *How much of my investments should be in the stock of the company where I work?* Many of us work for publicly traded companies and many of those companies include stock as a significant part of their employees' compensation.

The Random Walk theory says your company stock is just as likely to do well as the broader market, so there isn't much there to go on. But the concept of diversification is very important here. Having a large portion of your portfolio in a single company typically isn't recommended. A good rule of thumb is to limit the value of a single stock to 3-5% of your portfolio. If you accumulate 10% or more of your net worth in company stock, that seems too much.

Furthermore, diversification rears its head along another dimension. In addition to the stock holdings, the employee is "invested" in the company by being its employee. If things went poorly for the company the stock would go down but also the person's career could be at risk. That's a scary double whammy—losing money in the portfolio and losing earning potential. While it's hard to diversify away the risk of your employer struggling, it's easy to diversify the investment risk by selling the company stock and investing in other companies.

Yet many people struggle with this. The head follows financial theory and clearly says greater diversification is a good thing and recommends selling the company stock. The heart thinks of things like loyalty and keeping up with the Joneses as reasons to hold on to it.

Loyalty is important. Companies like employees owning their stock because collectively if a lot of their employees own stock, they are probably motivated to do better. But the employee doesn't really benefit from this. It's unlikely the individual is in a position to meaningfully impact the price of the stock, so the loyalty concept becomes a one-way street towards the company. The employee becomes overexposed with the company with little offsetting benefit.

The heart may also be influenced by the green-eyed monster, in conjunction with loss aversion. If a lot of the employee's peers are heavily invested in the company stock there becomes a perverse incentive to also be heavily invested. If the company does well, all the peers will become wealthy, and the person doesn't want to be left out, creating the incentive to similarly hold company stock. Of course, the opposite could happen and the company does poorly.

Now the psychology comes in. With hindsight, it would be best for the individual to invest in the company stock if it does well (and be rich along with her peers), but be diversified away from the company stock if it does poorly (and be rich when all the peers are poor). Obviously, this is a fantasy; people can't know what a stock will do before it happens. So it becomes a question of what would hurt more: not investing in the company stock when it does well (and have all the peers being richer) or not investing in the company stock when it does poorly (and being richer than all the peers). Humans feel worse with bad things (being poor when the peers are rich) than feel better for good things (being rich when the peers are poor).

As a result, people tend to accumulate company stock, listening to their heart, when they should be more diversified, listening to their head.

Paying off a mortgage

There is a whole chapter later in the book dedicated to debt. However, the emotional response many people have to debt allows it to fit here nicely as well.

There is a large segment of the investing population that is so anathema to debt that they employ the strategy of paying it off as quickly as possible, even if that means foregoing other investment options.

The heart and the head would agree on this with high-interest debt like credit card debt but they will disagree on lower-interest debt like a home mortgage. In fact, if your strategy is to maximize your overall net worth, paying off a mortgage quickly instead of saving money in a 401k is typically the wrong strategy. Yet so many people follow their heart when it says, "debt is bad, go full speed ahead and pay it off regardless of anything else."

At the end of that ride, your mortgage is paid off and that certainly feels great. Yet, mathematically, looking at historical returns, the more profitable strategy is to invest that extra money in stocks and pay off the mortgage at the regular cadence. Your heart loves not having debt hanging over you, but your head would rather have the higher net worth.

Emergency funds

A very common piece of advice investors get is that they should establish an emergency fund before they do anything else. People are told they need about 3-6 months of expenses in cash to deal with any emergencies that might come up. Based on those numbers, you'd need $20,000 to $30,000 in cash in an emergency fund.

On the surface the logic seems sound. No one wants to fall into financial straits due to an unforeseen challenge which would require them to make really tough choices, none of which are good. Yet, that advice is coming from your heart, not your head.

The first major miss with this advice is that your emergency fund does not need to be in cash. Cash, in a savings account, earns an abysmal interest rate compared to stocks or even bonds. Proponents of having a cash emergency fund will point to the fact that a savings account cannot lose value under any circumstance; if you have an emergency fund you don't want to face a situation where the value of the fund goes down just when you need it.

The second major miss is that 6 months' worth of expenses seems way too much; even three months seems like a lot. Obviously, a larger emergency fund is better than a smaller one, all other things being equal. But in real life, building an emergency fund comes at the cost of doing other things like saving in a 401k or paying off debt. There's no mathematical formula to say it should be 3 months but not 9 months. This is where life experience and observing others helps.

While your heart wants safety (the bigger emergency fund the better) and predictability (the more steady the investment the better), your head takes a much different approach. Your head will ask how many times you will truly have an emergency. By their very definition emergencies don't happen often. Everyone is different and it's impossible to predict the future. However, since I graduated college (about 25 years ago), I've maybe had two or three emergencies where I had to come up with at least $1,000 with less than one month's notice. Even our family's most significant financial setback, when my wife unexpectedly lost her job, came with a six-month severance so we had plenty of time to make the necessary adjustments.

Frequency is one thing (emergencies aren't that frequent), and severity is another. Six months of cash is a lot. The chances of a calamity that severe are remote. It's not that it can't happen, although I struggle to come up with a circumstance where I'd have zero income for six months and no ability to reduce my spending in the interim; rather it seems like overkill.

A more prudent choice is to build up an emergency fund while also doing other investments, most importantly your 401k or IRA. If an emergency happens right away, sometimes that happens. Also, your emergency fund can be in stocks. Investing in stocks offers a better return over the long-term, so that is a positive. The negative would occur if two unlikely events happened simultaneously—stocks went down and an emergency happened. Individually, each of those events is unlikely, especially over longer periods of time; combined, the chances of both occurring at the same time is tiny.

Chapter 10: *Debt*

Debt is a significant consideration for most people when they think about their personal finances. In absolute terms, debt is a negative. All other things being equal, you are better off having less debt than more debt. However, like many things in personal finance, there is nuance which makes that absolute statement—debt is bad so let's have none of it—not always the best approach.

As mentioned before, humans are really bad at finding middle grounds. This shortcoming rears its ugly head when it comes to debt. Most people know that really high-interest debt like credit cards is bad and should be avoided; that's absolutely true and those debts should be eliminated as quickly as possible. However, with that all-or-nothing mentality which humans naturally gravitate towards, many people take the approach that all debt is bad (probably true) and should be paid off immediately (probably not true).

It's all about interest rates

If you can get past the idea that all debt by definition is bad and should be avoided, then you can start thinking about it in terms of its costs, specifically the interest rate charged on the debt. Interest, as discussed in an earlier chapter is the amount charged every month to borrow the money.

Everyone acknowledges that high-interest debt (like credit cards) is bad and should be paid off as quickly as possible. But what about low-interest debt (like a mortgage or an auto loan)?

As an intellectual exercise, imagine you owe a debt with 0% interest. Would it make sense for you to pay that off faster than the minimum payments? Knowing you could invest that extra money in bonds that historically returns 4% or in stocks that historically return 10%, although with much more volatility, personal finance theory says that paying off that 0% debt quickly is a bad thing. Rather, you should pay off that interest-free debt as slowly as possible and invest any of the extra money that could have gone to eliminating that debt and invest it.

This creates a conundrum that people are so challenged by. When does debt, or more accurately the interest rate of debt, go from something that should be paid off immediately (like credit card debt) to something that should be paid off as slowly as possible (like that imaginary 0% loan)?

There's no exact answer. Like so many things this depends on a person's specific situation. Also, this is a head/heart situation where what is statistically best to maximize wealth may not be what allows the person to sleep best at night.

That said, the best approach is to identify all the debts you have and then rank order them by their interest rate from highest to lowest. Then draw a line where the interest rate changes from being "bad/pay that off right away" to "okay/take time to pay it off". The nearby table is an example of what this might look like.

Debt type	Typical interest rate
Credit card	20%
Car loan	8%
Student loan	5%
Mortgage	3%

Paying off debt is really investing for a guaranteed return

That approach begs the question: *When does debt go from one category (pay off right away) to the other (take your time)?*

Any debt you have accrues interest every day, every week, every month. Paying off that debt early allows you to avoid some of that interest in the future.

One way to think about it is that paying off debt is like having an investment with a guaranteed investment return. Imagine you have a loan with 15% interest, and then imagine you have an extra $100 that could either go towards paying off the loan or towards savings (that you would invest in some way). If you put that $100 towards the loan, you will save all the 15% interest that was being charged on that $100. If the idea of reducing your expenses or increasing your income are two sides of the same coin, then saving that 15% on interest should be seen as the same as earning a 15% return.

That becomes a profound concept. Putting the $100 towards your debt saves you 15% interest, which can be seen the same as giving you a 15% return. Furthermore, saving that 15% interest is guaranteed. If you pay off some of your loan, there is an absolute certainty that you won't be charged interest on that money. That begins to look like a risk-free return.

Going back to the **Risk and Reward** chapter, we know that higher returns come with higher risk. And we know savings accounts which are 100% guaranteed usually have a low return, like 1%; bonds have low risk and average returns around 4%; stocks are very risky and have average returns around 10%. Your paying off that 15% loan early allows you a guaranteed return (like a savings account) but with a really high rate (like a stock). That is as good as it gets. There is no investment out there that offers a guaranteed return of 15%.

You can apply this idea to all your debt. Paying off high debts like credit cards and car loans are an easy decision. There is no investment out there that combines a guaranteed return with such a high return.

As you move down your list to lower interest loans, it becomes murkier. Maybe your student loan has a 5% interest rate. Paying that off early guarantees a 5% return which is a bit better than bonds, but not near as good as stocks. This is a harder decision based on your feelings regarding risk. Would you prefer a guaranteed 5% return by paying off your loan, or would you prefer an expected 10% return with stocks knowing sometimes it will be higher than that but other times lower than that?

Go all the way to the bottom of your list and you might have a mortgage at a 3% interest rate (in actuality, since mortgage interest is tax deductible, it might be more accurate to think of that 3% loan as a 2.5% loan). Paying off a 30-year mortgage earlier doesn't offer near the return that you could expect from holding stocks for 30-years.

There's no strict value to use here, but a good rule of thumb seems to be 4-5%. Any loans with interest higher than that should be prioritized when you have extra money because it's hard to find a guaranteed return that can compete with that. Any loans with interest lower than that allow for the opportunity to take that extra money and invest it in something that will give, or maybe more accurately "probably give", a higher return.

Chapter 11: *Asset Allocation*

Asset Allocation is probably the most important yet least understood aspects of personal finance. The idea of asset allocation is looking at what percentage of your portfolio goes into different asset types. For most investors, there are really only three asset types to consider—cash, bonds, and stocks. More sophisticated investors may expand that list, but even then there isn't clear evidence that doing so provides higher returns.

In a lot of ways Asset Allocation is the culmination of all the elements of financial theory that have been discussed heretofore. Concepts like Risk and Return, Time Horizon, Diversification all come together here as the rubber hits the road and you determine what investments to make with your portfolio.

High stakes

The importance of Asset Allocation is so important because it is what is driving the level of returns you get. With Asset Allocation you are picking how much of your nest egg goes into stocks (high risk, high return), bonds (low risk, low return), and cash (no risk, minimal return). Over the long term, the higher your allocation of stocks, the higher your return should be. Of course, as has been mentioned ad nauseum in previous chapters, those higher returns come with higher volatility and uncertainty.

Asset Allocation is deceptively powerful, which means that even small differences in Asset Allocation can result in huge differences to your net worth over longer periods of time. Imagine the difference between one portfolio with a 50% asset allocation for stocks and 50% for bonds, and compare it to a second portfolio with 60% stocks and 40% bonds. There is a 10% difference between those two scenarios. It seems trivial.

Yet the seemingly small difference is profound when it is compounded over time. The 60/40 portfolio will out-perform the 50/50 portfolio by 13% (assume that the average return for stocks is 10% and for bonds 4%). If each portfolio started at $100,000 and grew over 40 years, the 60/40 portfolio would be worth about $2.7 million while the 50/50 portfolio would be worth about $2.3 million. That is about a $400,000 difference, and bear in mind that you started with $100,000. Those are high stakes indeed.

There are very few other investing concepts that have that large an impact. Diversification doesn't. Choosing between a Roth IRA and a Traditional IRA doesn't. Paying off your mortgage quickly doesn't. Investing in your 401k probably does, but that's about it. Asset Allocation is really, really important.

No clear "right" answer

Making Asset Allocation particularly vexing is there is no clearly right or clearly wrong answer. We know that more stocks lead to higher returns, but they also entail more risk. The balance of risk and return would suggest that most investors should be somewhere in the middle, not at 100% stocks but not at 0% stocks either.

There is no mathematical formula that tells an investor precisely where between 0% and 100% they should be. In fact, there's no real consensus among investment professionals either; if you have 20 financial planners in a room, you'll probably get 20 different answers to what your optimal Asset Allocation should be.

This is in stark contrast to many other concepts of personal finance which nearly every credible finance professional can agree on:

- *Should you pay off your 20% credit card debt as quickly as possible?* Absolutely—100% agreement.
- *If I know my child will go to college, should I save money in a 529?* Yes—95% agreement.
- *Should I stop contributing to my 401k to pay off my mortgage faster?* Almost all financial planners will say that's a bad idea—90% agreement.
- *Should I be all invested in a single stock?* No—100% agreement.
- *Do stocks do better than bonds over the long term?* Yes—99% agreement.

- *How much of my portfolio should be in stocks versus bonds?* Ummm.

This certainly makes this critical decision a daunting one.

Changes over time

To add further challenge and confusion to the Asset Allocation decision is the fact that it should change over time. As you get older, you get closer to needing the money you have saved for retirement (or for college expenses or whatever long-term savings goals you have).

A universally accepted idea is the closer you come to needing the money from your portfolio, the less risky your investments should be. If you're young and won't need your retirement savings for decades, riskier investments with higher returns are appropriate because you have time to ride out any bad years. However, if you're on the cusp of retirement and will need that money in a couple years or less, you would want to have your investments in less risky investments so you avoid the doomsday scenario of a market crash right before you withdraw your money.

No one agrees on exactly what your asset allocation should be when you have a long investment horizon and no one agrees on what it should be as you get closer to liquidation. Yet, pretty much everyone agrees that the percentage of stocks should decrease over time. Also, no one agrees on how fast that decrease should be.

In light of all those varying viewpoints, there are a couple places we can look to for guidance. There are several mutual funds out there that were designed to address this very issue. They are called Target Date Funds, and basically they take the date you want to have access to the money you invest, and they do the asset allocation for you. Illustrating this concept, as that target date gets closer, they shift away from stocks and towards bonds.

The nearby table shows the Asset Allocation that Vanguard uses for their line of Target Date Funds as of the time of this writing. For example, VTIVX is designed for investors who will want their money in 20 years. The Asset Allocation for this fund is 84% stocks and 16% bonds.

Estimated years to withdraw	% Stocks	% Bonds
0—access money now (VTTVX)	53%	46%
10 (VTTHX)	70%	30%
20 (VTIVX)	84%	16%
30 (VFFVX)	90%	10%
40 (VLXVX)	90%	10%

This is what Vanguard, either the largest or second largest asset management firm in the world (depending on how you measure it), thinks is appropriate. However, reasonable people can disagree. Personally, I think 10% in bonds for someone with a 40-year time horizon is too much; I would put that at zero (more on this in a second). But no one, me included, would disagree with the trend that the percentage of stocks should go down as the time horizon shortens.

There are some interesting things to note. First, and this is really important, even if you are in retirement and actively withdrawing your money, Vanguard recommends 53% of your portfolio be in stocks. This is a huge Asset Allocation concept that so many people get wrong. Many people, probably listening to their heart, think that they need to be completely out of stocks during retirement.

Earlier we saw the profound impact that a 10% difference in asset allocation could have. Imagine a 53% difference over a long retirement. That's not to say that Vanguard is right or wrong, but it does speak to how important this is.

As unique as you are

Each of us is unique and that requires a unique investing strategy which is appropriate to our particular situation. That certainly applies to Asset Allocation. The percentage of your portfolio that should be in stocks (already an impossible question to answer) is going to be different from other people, many of who seem just like you.

The most obvious difference is your time horizon as illustrated above. To a large degree, the financial services industry has taken care of this dimension with their target date funds. But there are a lot of other differences that are important.

- *Homeownership*—Owning a home (and the associated equity that goes with it) would suggest a higher percentage of stocks than someone without any home equity.
- *Defined benefit pension*—Getting a pension from your job tends to sit outside the Asset Allocation decision because those are not funds you invest; you just collect the money at the appropriate age. That said, having a pension would suggest that the other investments you do have should have a higher percentage of stocks.
- *Life-expectancy*—No one likes to think about their own mortality, but those with a longer life expectancy (based on genetics, previous health issues, etc.) should tend to have a higher percentage of stocks.

Those are a few that came to mind quickly, and I am sure you could come up with many more. The point is every one of us is different. Some characteristics that would make me want to be more conservative than others will push me to have a higher bond allocation, while other characteristics will make me want to be more aggressive.

Put all those in the mix and it's hard to say exactly what my Asset Allocation should be. The numbers from Vanguard serve as a good guide, but that is all they are—a guide. Your Asset Allocation should reflect your unique circumstances.

Hidden bonds

This chapter opened with the idea that Asset Allocation is important (it is) and that most people get it wrong. This is controversial, but I believe most people get it wrong because they allocate much more to bonds than they should (I admit that many highly regarded financial professionals will strongly disagree with me on this).

First, people tend to be much more conservative than they should, especially in retirement. Second, people tend to not consider their entire financial picture when looking at Asset Allocation for the portfolio.

Social Security is a good example. Most Americans will get a monthly check from the US government when we are retired. In a lot of ways, that monthly check looks and feels like a bond. If it's a bond (and mathematically a fairly large bond for most of us) then it should be taken into account when thinking about how to invest your other money.

An average Social Security payment might be $3,000 per month ($36,000 annually) when someone turns 70. Using some simple math, someone could buy a 4% government bond and they would need to buy about $900,000 in bonds to get interest equivalent to $3,000 monthly. Obviously, there are differences between these two examples (you may outlive the bond or you may die well before it matures being the most important), but it gives you a sense for the "value" of your Social Security benefits.

If it looks like a duck and quacks like a duck, then you should treat it like a duck. Your Social Security is a *monthly amount of money you get that is guaranteed by the US government*. You could use those exact words to describe a US Treasury Bond. Now, incorporate that idea that your Social Security is really like a $900,000 bond. Add the benefits of your spouse if that's your situation and that is $1,800,000.

In this light, how does that impact your decision on how to invest your 401k or IRA? It should embolden most to be more aggressive and increase the percentage of stocks, knowing you already have a lot of money in something that is very "bond-like". Yet, many people don't think about their Social Security (or home equity or pension) like this, and they go with a lower stock allocation and the lower long-term returns associated with that decision.

Chapter 12: *Retirement Accounts*

All the theoretical knowledge about personal finance is important only to the degree it is used to help build wealth. The rubber hits the road when money is saved and invested. For the vast, vast majority of Americans those investments are going to be made in retirement accounts. Accounts like 401k and IRAs are typically the only investment account needed for most Americans. Investment professionals can debate this, but I would think in most situations a person making up to $150,000 or with a net worth of less than $1 million would not need to use any account other than his 401k or IRA.

401k/403b

For most people, their 401k is the single best investment vehicle they have access to. The tax-deferral feature (avoiding paying taxes now, but paying taxes when you withdraw) can be worth tens of thousands of dollars. Most companies offer a match and that can be worth hundreds of thousands of dollars.

A 401k also has an extremely high contribution limit compared to similar types of investments like IRAs. In 2024 a person can invest up to $23,000 each year in her 401k (these limits typically increase over time due to inflation); if the person is older than 50, that increases to $30,000. That's a lot of money and most investors won't reach those limits. If the 401k is the best single investment account you have access to, then that means it's the only investment account you need until you hit that $23,000 cap. In the vast majority of circumstances, your 401k should be your primary workhorse for investing. That makes things much simpler.

A 403b is functionally equivalent to a 401k. 401k accounts are used for people who work for for-profit companies, while 403b accounts are for people who work for governments. That said, the concepts discussed for 401k accounts almost universally apply to public-sector employees and their 403b accounts.

IRAs and Roth IRAs

After a 401k, an IRA (either Traditional or Roth) is often your best option. They aren't as good as a 401k because they don't offer a match and they have a lower contribution limit; you can contribute $7,000 annually to an IRA ($8,000 if you're 50 or older) which is quite a bit less than is the case for a 401k. Also, the government has placed income limits on those who can use an IRA. Traditional IRAs lose their tax advantage when your income exceeds the $80,000 range; you cannot contribute to a Roth IRA if your income exceeds the $160,000 range. There are no income limits for a 401k. That said, if you don't have access to a 401k or if you have already maxed it out, IRAs are a really good investment tool.

If you decide to use an IRA it begs the question: *Should I do a traditional IRA or a Roth IRA?* To some degree the question is answered for you by the income limits. If you make more than around $80,000, you can't get the tax benefit of a Traditional IRA, so there is no real point in using it, making you better off using a Roth IRA. If your income exceeds $160,000 then you can't use a Roth IRA either.

For incomes less than $80,000 you have the choice between a Traditional and a Roth, and the math is a bit ambiguous. The main advantage of a Traditional IRA is you don't pay taxes now, presumably when your income is in a higher tax bracket. However, if your income is below $80,000 it is already in a lower tax bracket, so the major benefit is muted.

At the upper end of the range, $60-80k, the math says it's better to do a Traditional IRA. At lower income levels your tax rate is already so low that it's hard to imagine meaningful tax benefits for a Traditional IRA compared to the absolute guarantee that your gains won't be taxed that a Roth IRA offers. You're splitting hairs here, but if you wanted a simple answer, I would say always go with a Roth just to make things easy. You might be leaving some tax savings on the table if your income is at the higher range, but there is something to be said for ease and simplicity.

Chapter 13: *Savings for College*

Saving for college is one of the important financial goals that most people have. In my experience speaking with many families, it ranks second only to having a comfortable retirement. Given the extremely high costs (and getting higher and higher every year) of higher-education, this is a subject that warrants considerable attention when thinking about personal finance and your investing strategy.

529 is a no-brainer

A 529 is an investment account specifically created to save for educational expenses. Initially, when the law creating 529s was passed in the late 1990s, they were meant only for higher education like college tuition. Since then, they have expanded greatly to cover anything remotely related to education, including expenses while the person is still a child (like private high school tuition).

The benefit of a 529 is primarily the tax treatment of returns, as discussed in an earlier chapter. This applies to both dividends that occur while the money grows in the account as well as any capital gains when the investments are sold and spent on educational expenses. Put simply, there are no taxes on any of those returns. In this way, a 529 acts very similarly to a Roth IRA. You save money after taxes, and any gains on that money over the years is tax free.

Even better, in some states, the money you save is pretax rather than after tax. This applies to state taxes and not federal taxes, so it's not nearly as good as it sounds, but that is another huge benefit.

The whole point of investing is to get more money out than you put in. Under most circumstances that gain will be taxed. Not with 529s. If you know you're going to have educational expenses of some type, then it becomes a no-brainer to use a 529.

There is a downside to 529s in that the money has to be used on educational expenses. Pulling the money out and spending it on non-educational expenses eliminates the tax benefit and also incurs penalties. Theoretically, if a family saves money in a 529 and then their child has no educational expenses, they would fall in this scenario.

That said, there is a lot of flexibility which makes that scenario not nearly as bad as it might first seem. First, 529 money can be spent on any educational expenses. If college isn't right for the child, maybe she'll go to trade school or a vocational program or something else. Any of those other options are eligible for 529 money.

Second, if the child does attend college but has scholarships which reduce the cost of attendance (a good problem to have), the amount of money equal to the scholarships can be withdrawn without penalty. Third, the 529 money is extremely transferable between family members. If a family has multiple kids and one doesn't go to college but the other does, the first child's 529 money can be transferred to the second child. This can extend widely to include siblings, children, cousins, grandchildren, and many more.

Definitely there is some risk associated with not being able to spend your child's 529 money and incurring a penalty, but this seems really low. The benefits, which are huge, are nearly 100% going to happen. This makes 529s an absolute must-do when it comes to saving for educational expenses.

Monthly savings goals

Tactically, there is always a question of how much a person should save for their kids' educational expenses. This depends on many factors so the answer is: "it depends." However, there are some good rules of thumb.

To keep things simple, looking at two factors will get you a fairly accurate answer to the question: *How much do I need to save each month to pay for my child's higher education?*

- *__How expensive the college is:__* Tuition for higher education varies widely. Trade schools and community colleges are extremely affordable (maybe the best bargain in higher education). In-state tuition for public colleges average to about $25,000 per year. Private colleges or out-of-state tuition for public colleges average to about $70,000 annually. Obviously, the more expensive the school, the more a parent will need to save.

- **_When in the child's life you start saving:_** As with every element of investing, the earlier you start, the better. This is driven by three key reasons. Starting earlier gives you more time to save. Starting when a child is born gives 18 years (216 months) versus when a child turns 8 and you only have 10 years to save (120 months). Splitting up the cost 216 times makes for a much more affordable monthly investment than splitting it up only 120 times.

  Second, starting earlier allows more time for the investments to grow. Compounding returns over 18 years are substantially higher than over 10 years.

  Third, starting earlier gives the money a longer time horizon which allows for more aggressive investments (with higher returns) early on. Any responsible 529 strategy would have the investments be conservative when it comes time to take the money out.   However, if you start early enough you can have some time when the investments have 18 years to grow and you can invest in more stocks than you would if you only had 10 years left. We discussed extensively about the higher returns associated with more aggressive asset allocation when the time frame allows.

All that said, using some simple assumptions and a spreadsheet, nearby is a table that shows a guide to how much you would need to save each month to pay for a child's higher education.

Child's age when you start saving	Trade school ($5,000)	In-state Public ($25,000)	Private/ Out-of-state ($70,000)
0—at birth	$40	$201	$560
5	$63	$316	$882
10	$104	$520	$1,456
15	$192	$960	$2,688
18—starting college	$417	$2,085	$5,838

The math here is fairly simple, so you can figure out other scenarios like paying for half of the child's in-state tuition by taking half of the monthly number. If you want pay for 25% of the tuition, take 25% of the number and so on.

Prioritize your retirement over their education

Some of those numbers can get pretty high, and that is just for one child. A family with a couple children that are going to college can make those numbers really daunting. Given there is only so much money to go around, and most families' top two financial goals are saving for retirement and saving for their children's higher education, it begs the question: _Should I prioritize saving for my child's education or for my retirement?_

The answer here is easy, yet it sounds harsh: Prioritize saving for your retirement before you put a dime away for someone else's education. This is another one of those head versus heart situations. Our parental instincts always tell us to sacrifice for our children. That is the very essence of parenthood. Yet, that is the exact wrong thing to do.

Similar to how on airlines they say if the oxygen masks pop out of the ceiling, you should put your mask on first before you help anyone else with their mask (even before helping your own children with their masks). The thinking is if you pass out because you're helping someone else, everyone loses. You're passed out so that's bad for you, but also since you're passed out you can't help anyone else out, so that's bad for them too. No one wins.

The analogy applies very well to investing when picking between saving for your retirement or for your children's education. With education, there are a lot of options— many types of student loans, the student working while in school and over the summer, going to a less expensive school (similar to mutual fund fees, there's not a ton of robust evidence that more expensive schools lead to better outcomes), and on and on.

Compared to all those options for college students, there really aren't that many for people approaching retirement. There's no such thing as a supplemental retirement loan. Even thinking of this from the child's perspective, a child would probably be better off with a non-impoverished parent than with an expensive degree. This is definitely a time where the right answer is the selfish answer.

Chapter 14: *Other Investment Types*

Throughout this book, we've only discussed two main types of investments—stocks and bonds. If you're generous you could include cash as a third, but that's really it. Of course, in the investing world there are many, many others. That begs the questions: *What are the other asset classes and what role should other asset classes play in my portfolio?*

Gold

Long before there were ever stocks or bonds, the original investment was gold. Just like stocks and bonds, gold is an investment. The idea is to buy it and have it increase in value. Historically, it seems to have been a good one—back in 1950 an ounce of gold was worth about $375 and today it's worth about $2000.

However, there is a major difference between gold as an investment compared to stocks and bonds (as we discussed in an earlier chapter). Gold is a store of value. If you buy gold it doesn't "do" anything. It just sits in a vault collecting dust until you sell it to someone else.

That's very different from stocks and bonds. When you buy a stock that money "does" something. It builds a factory that produces stuff or it buys a car that delivers goods or on and on. Whatever it is, it's creating something of value, making the pie bigger. That is a huge difference compared to gold, and it's a huge advantage that stocks and bonds have over gold. You actually see that play out by looking at the long-term investment performance of gold versus stocks.

Statistically speaking, gold gives an investor more diversification than probably any other asset. In fact, gold is one of the few asset classes that is negatively correlated with stocks (for you fellow statistics nerds, the correlation is about -0.12). Basically, that means when stocks go up gold tends to go down, and when stocks go down gold tends to go up.

Over the short term, that's probably a pretty good thing, especially if you want to make sure that your overall portfolio doesn't become too volatile. In fact, that's one of the reasons gold is sometimes called "portfolio insurance". It helps protect the value of your portfolio if stocks start falling, since gold tends to go up when stocks go down.

However, over the long-term, that's super counter-productive. We all know that over longer periods of time, stocks have a very strong upward trend. If gold is negatively correlated with stocks, and if over the long-term stocks nearly always go up, then that means that over the long-term gold nearly always goes down.

Price of gold over time (the grey bars represent US recessions)

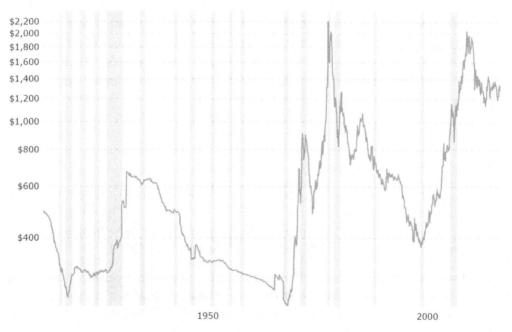

That doesn't seem right, but the data is solid. Look back to 1950: an ounce of gold cost $375 while it's about $2,000 at the time of writing this book. That's an increase of about 250% which might seem pretty good, but over 70 years that's actually pretty bad, about 2% per year. Compare that to stocks which we know have about an 10% average return.

Just to add salt in the wound, inflation has been about 3.5% since 1950. Mathematically, gold has lost purchasing power over the long term.

Historically, gold has performed best when stocks have performed worst. The nearby table shows the price of gold going back the early 1900s. The major peaks for gold corresponded to periods of major financial collapse—1930s with the Great Depression, 1970s with stagflation and oil shocks, and 2008 with the Great Recession.

Over the short-term there may be some diversification value with gold as an investment, but over the long-term gold is not a good investment.

Commodities

The story for commodities is very similar to that of gold. Both are stores of value where money is made or lost based on the price movements. This starts to look much more like gambling and much less like investing because the whole investing strategy boils down to whether people will pay more for something tomorrow versus today. This is driven by very unpredictable things like war or bad weather or broad macroeconomic trends. While stocks have a strong upward trend because they are making the pie bigger, commodities are just a zero-sum game.

That alone would make commodities not a good long-term investment. However, this is further compounded by the fact that investing in commodities, by its very nature, is a short-term endeavor. There is tremendous value in having a long-term investing perspective with stocks as we have discussed extensively. All commodities tend to be short term because many go bad. Most commodities are traded as futures or options which have expirations on the scale of months or a couple years at most. That means you either need to win or lose on that investment within that very short time period.

As such, similar to gold, commodities may provide diversity in the short-term, but they have proven to be poor investments over the long term.

Foreign Currency

Foreign currency investing looks similar to commodities investing in a couple ways. Typically, it's a short-term strategy since, like commodities, most foreign currency trading is done with options and futures which are built for short-term use. Also, similar to gold and commodities, foreign currency doesn't create value in and of itself, so investing in it becomes a zero-sum game where you're guessing if someone else will pay more for it in the future.

What makes foreign currencies different, and much riskier, is that its value is driven by interest rates set by central banks (as discussed in a previous chapter). If a country raises its interest rates, its currency will appreciate; if it lowers its interest rates its currency will depreciate. An investment here is really a bet on what central banks will do relative to each other. Consistently making accurate predictions here is near impossible for normal investors, so this becomes much less like investing and much more like gambling.

A final point against investing in foreign currencies that applies to Americans, is that there are very few examples of other currencies that have performed better than the US dollar over the long term. Americans, by definition, have US dollars as their default currency. To invest in foreign currencies means selling US dollars for something else with the belief that the other currency will do better than the US dollar.

The US dollar is the reserve currency of the world. It's the most widely used and widely traded currency. For all those reasons and many more, the US dollar retains its strength much better than any other currency.

The world is littered with examples of currencies whose value has cratered—Germany in post-World War II, the Russian Ruble in 1998 and again in 2022, the Argentine Peso almost every year, most countries in Africa. Our instinct would be to try to diversify some of that risk away, and that may be appropriate if you live in those countries and hold those currencies. However, for most Americans there is not that need, making foreign currencies a poor long-term investment.

Real estate

Real estate investing is a huge asset class, probably bigger than stocks. Here, there are two ways to invest: passively and actively.

Passive real estate investing is very similar to investing in stocks. You give your money to someone else, and they invest in real estate. You get your share of the income and when it is time to sell the property you get your share of that as well. This can be done on a very large scale to the point that there are publicly traded companies that all they do is invest in real estate. There is an entire subclass of stocks called Real Estate Investment Trusts (REITs) that do exactly this. For these companies, investing in real estate is no different than investing in any other stock.

Scaled down, you can give your money to a smaller company or even a friend to make those investments. As can be imagined, the potential upside can be considerably higher as is the risk. Also, the costs of maintaining this type of investment are much higher.

The other option is active real estate investing where you purchase property for rental. The concept is fundamentally the same—you buy the property and you get a share of the income (similar to a dividend) and a share of the profit when the property is sold (similar to a capital gain). Based on historic averages, the return from rental properties is significantly higher than for stocks, but that comes with a catch. Here you cease to become an investor and you become a landlord.

Being an investor requires very little work and typically very low costs. Being a landlord is a bona fide job. It can be outsourced but that will dramatically reduce the return. Also, it can involve significant costs and risks, especially if there become problems with the tenant.

Also, owning rental properties is a very undiversified investment. It is similar to a very large investment in a single stock. If things go well then the gains are much larger, but there is also exposure to risks that multiple investments would diversify away. Additionally, stocks are very liquid; if you needed to sell stocks to get money tomorrow that is fairly easy to do. Selling a rental property is a slow and expensive undertaking.

The upside to rental properties is enormous, but it's really not an investment as much as a job. The concepts that are important to investing like diversification, lower costs, and government laws to protect investors all go out the window with rental properties. That doesn't make them bad, but it just makes them different.

Private equity

Private equity is very similar to investing in stocks, but it does so for companies that are not publicly traded. You could invest in Apple by buying shares of Apple stock. This is fairly easy to do and the costs are quite low.

If instead of Apple you wanted to invest in a company that is not publicly traded (SpaceX, Cargill, and Mars candy are examples of large private companies in the US), you can do so but only via private equity. Basically, those private companies go to investing companies seeking capital. Those investing companies raise money from investors and then give that to the private company. The ultimate outcome is the same as with public companies but there is a middleman (or several middlemen) and the process is much more complex.

Among investing professionals there is active debate as to whether or not this type of investment is appropriate for ordinary investors. The law is complex, but generally a person must be considered a "sophisticated investor" as defined by the US government in order to invest in private equity. The criteria a person must meet is to have a net worth of over $1 million or to make $200,000 annually.

Whether private equity makes a good investment is hotly debated by financial professionals. What is not debated is that these types of investments have extremely high fees. An index mutual fund might charge 0.05% annually; a common fee structure for private equity would see fees of over 2% annually.

Less clear is if private equity out performs stocks, much less if they outperform stocks after taking into account those higher fees. There are countless studies falling on both sides of the argument. For most normal investors, this is probably not an appropriate investment.

Cryptocurrencies

Cryptocurrencies have emerged as the darling or the devil of the investing world. Their stories are captivating. Bitcoin, the largest and most prevalent cryptocurrency, went from a value of $200 ten years ago to about $60,000 today. That type of meteoric rise can't help but generate interest.

In truth, the concept of crypto is very appealing. It is separated from any government or central bank, so it is not subject political gamesmanship from people trying to get reelected. Also, its supply is predetermined so there will never be rapid inflation due to a huge increase in the money supply. Intellectually those are appealing, and it could very well be that in 20 years or so crypto might become much more important than it is today.

However, in the here and now, crypto is an investing novelty. First, it has no use in and of itself because you can't use it anywhere as a currency. Currencies are meant to be stores of value that let you buy stuff you want, but you can't pay for your groceries or your cell phone bill or the babysitter with crypto. That relegates it to something similar to gold; the difference is that gold has been around for millennia and is extremely well understood and trusted.

Second, and even more challenging for crypto is that it is difficult to trade. There are only a handful of trading platforms through which you can own crypto. And those that do exist have a horrible track record of safety, going back to the hacking scandals of Mt Gox and even more recently the FTX meltdown. This contrasts sharply with stocks where brokerage firms are plentiful and safe.

Crypto may be the shiny new toy in the investing world, but gimmicks are not meant to be a meaningful part of your portfolio. Maybe over the coming decades it will solve some of its shortcomings and then deserve a role in your investing strategy, but that day is not today.

Chapter 15: *Avoid Blunders*

There is a common refrain in sports that *the team that wins most often is not the team that has the most good plays, but it is the team that avoids the most bad plays.* In football, you don't need to throw 50-yard touchdown passes, but rather avoid turnovers. In baseball you don't need more homeruns, but rather fewer throwing errors.

That can equally apply to investing. Your personal finance journey is a long and slow one. Also, it's one that is built for you to win; remember that historically stocks return 10% on average. You don't need to strive for the investment that doubles in a year (although those sure are nice), but rather you need to avoid the blunders that in a quick moment will negate years or decades of hard work.

Also, it is critically important that you make the distinction between a poor-performing investment and a blunder. Picking an investment that goes down is not a failing; those things happen. Over your investing career, you will certainly pick some investments that do poorly, especially over shorter periods of time. Welcome to the world of investing.

Blunders are different. Blunders are self-inflicted (and quite frankly, easily avoided) mistakes investors make, usually in pursuit of quick and large returns that ultimately reduce the overall worth of their portfolios.

Set reasonable expectations

We have spent a ton of time discussing reasonable expectations for the returns of different investment types, especially stocks. Historically stocks have returned 8-10% annually. When you develop your plan, you will need to make assumptions regarding the returns you will get. Resist the temptation to assume returns higher than those long-term averages.

Everyone wants to be able to have a higher net worth. Everyone wants to be able to save less for the future so they can spend more today. Mathematically that can be easily accomplished on a spreadsheet just by increasing your expected return from 8% to 10% to 12% to 14%. Yet that is a very risky game that exposes you to considerable risk.

Perhaps you'll get lucky and your investing timeframe will coincide with a decades long bull market driven by transformational innovations like the 1980s and 1990s. But luck is not a strategy. If your financial plan requires returns above the historic averages, then you need to redo your plan. Either save more, save for longer, or spend less once you start harvesting your investments.

Do not chase high returns

There are a million investments out there, and by definition some of those will have higher returns and some will have lower returns. Obviously, every investor would want higher returns, so it is very tempting to imagine "What if I had invested in that one that did really well?" Avoid the temptation.

This is probably the single most thoroughly researched concept in all of personal finance. The data has unequivocally shown that investments that have done well in the recent past do not have a greater chance of doing well in the future.

Yet humans seem hardwired to pursue these strategies. Bitcoin has exploded in value over the past 10 few years; since we want that same performance in the future it's tempting to dive into Bitcoin now. The same thing can apply to Nvidia or Turkish stocks.

Those winning stories make the headlines and generate the excitement, but know that as often as not, those high fliers crash and burn. In the 1990s it was Japanese stocks after an incredible multiple-decades long run. In the 2000s Circuit City went bankrupt after being one of the best performing stocks of the 1980s.

Sometimes you'll get lucky and catch an investment that rockets to the moon. That's really fun and you'll enjoy telling all your friends how smart you were to invest in that. But always remember that such investments are just luck. Keeping a broadly diversified portfolio over the long term will give you the greatest chance to reap strong returns.

Don't throw Hail Mary's at the end of the game

As you get close to the end of your investing journey, you may find yourself in a situation where you are tempted to take on really risky investments later because your overall portfolio isn't as large as you would want it to be. In football, at the end of the game losing teams often throw a Hail Mary pass which results in interceptions much more often than in touchdowns. In hockey, at the end of the game losing teams often pull their goalie to get an extra attacker which results in goals against them much more often than goals for them.

As you approach the end, you may find that you haven't accumulated as much as you would have liked. Certainly, that would be disappointing. Many would be tempted to remedy this by seeking higher returns. This is a very risky proposition.

A central theme of this book is that an investor can only obtain higher returns by taking on riskier investments. Another central theme is that as an investor gets older and closer to harvesting his investments, his portfolio should become less risky. Trying to drive higher returns towards the end of your investing timeline runs counter to both of these. You would take on more and more risk when you have less and less time.

The solution, as undesirable as it may seem, is to accept the lower value of the portfolio as a given. You can increase your investments by saving more in the years you still have. You can forestall retirement, continuing to work and save for longer. You can accept that you will have less to spend in retirement. All three of those options involve sacrifice along some dimension. None of those options are particularly appealing, and it would certainly be more attractive to find a solution that does not entail any of those sacrifices, but such free lunches do not exist.

Understand that things go up and down

Investments by their very nature are unpredictable. While the data show that stocks do go up 10% per year on average, those two words "on average" are incredibly important.

Over your investing lifetime, you will have many years where stocks go down. Just to humble you, the investing gods may run a few of those bad years together to really test your faith. Don't waiver, no matter how bleak things may look at any given time.

In my investing lifetime (since 1995) there have been four major stock meltdowns—the Dot-Com Bubble of 2000, the Great Recession of 2008, the Covid Collapse in 2020, and the Inflation Slide of 2022. In each case, the falls were steep and unrelenting. Some were quick while others lasted years. Beyond those most extreme examples, there were other painful times in the market—the end of 2018, January of 2016, and July of 2011—just to name a couple others.

Every time, in the midst of the market turmoil, it was easy to capitulate, panic at the sights of months or years of savings vaporizing in the matter of a couple days, and want to abandon stocks. Resist the urge. Things like that happen. Stocks will go up and down. That cycle will happen several times over your investing lifetime.

Keeping the faith and maintaining a steady investing approach (in line with fundamentals like Asset Allocation and your Time Horizon) is almost always the best strategy. Bonus points if you have the internal fortitude to view those times, in the midst of the chaos, as a buying opportunity and invest when the stocks are selling on the cheap.

Avoid complexity

The entire ecosystem of investing is enormous, and it can be enormously complex. As we have discussed, there are innumerable investing products out there designed to fill every niche an investor could possibly need. In fact it extends beyond "need"; there are countless products that fulfill needs that the vast majority of investors do not have. These products are created, supported by some slick marketing, and often promoted by advisors who get considerable fees to push them on their clients.

A common thread here is that the more complex a financial product is, the less likely it is that typical investor will understand it, the higher the fees are for the middlemen, and ultimately the less it will support you achieving your personal finance goals.

Bonds and stocks are fairly easy to understand. Beyond that, mutual funds are a touch more complex, but still fairly simple. Those products have fairly low costs and are highly appropriate for the vast, vast majority of investors.

Credit-default swaps defy a simple explanation. Even investments like variable annuities, options and futures, and whole life insurance entail a fair amount of complexity. On top of that complexity, those types of investments are laden with fees. A common investor doesn't need any of those. The overwhelming majority of investors could accomplish everything they need with a US-equity index mutual fund, and international-equity index mutual fund, a bond mutual fund, and a money market account. Anything beyond that burdens an investor with more risk and higher fees than is appropriate.

Put trust in those who earn it

Throughout life, trust is a tricky thing; this is especially true with investing. If you do all your investing yourself, you'll never have that issue. However, if you do work with a financial advisor (an earlier chapter noted the positives and negatives of such a decision), it is critical that you work with someone who you can trust.

A good first step is to only work with someone who holds herself as a "fiduciary". That is a legal term that requires the financial advisor to put your interests ahead of everyone else's, including her own. It's sad that such a term is necessary, but it is. Without the fiduciary label, the advisor could recommend actions that are more in her best interests than yours. Perhaps that is making an investment that offers her higher fees; perhaps it is steering you towards an investment with people who she is trying to impress or "get in with".

Unfortunately, while the "fiduciary" designation is a start, it is not enough by itself. If the advisor was not acting in your best interests, it would probably require a legal remedy. That's a whole can of worms you want to avoid.

It's better just to make sure the advisor you do work with is trustworthy from the start. Knowing who to trust and how much to trust them is no simple proposition, and it is well beyond the scope of this book. Personal recommendations, research of government databases, longevity, and many other factors should be helpful. No matter how you do it, if you entrust someone else to help you with your personal finances, make sure they deserve your trust.

Chapter 16: *Top 5 Financial To-Dos*

There are so many things to think about in personal finance, and it's easy to understand why it can get so overwhelming for so many people. Unfortunately, in the face of this, many will just throw their hands up and do nothing, and that will often lead to disastrous financial consequences.

But personal finance, like so many other things can use the 80/20 rule; you can probably get 80% of the benefit by doing 20% of the stuff. If you were only going to do five things with your personal finances, what would they be?

1. Figure out your debt situation

Debt is a common feature of most people's financial situation, particularly for younger people who may have graduated with school loans or who may have slipped into credit card debt early on when they weren't making much money or who may have had to take out loans for a car or furniture when they were getting started. At its worst, debt can be an absolute albatross that makes building a strong financial future impossible.

Take an inventory of all your debt. On a spreadsheet make a list of what you owe to everyone, and next to it list the interest rate associated with it. Then sort it by interest rate, with the highest rates on top of the list and the lowest at the bottom.

Put a plan in place to pay off that debt. As we discussed, if the debt has a low rate like a mortgage or a subsidized rate like on a car loan or an interest free rate, there is no need to pay that off faster than the normal payment. However, for higher-rate debt, you should have a plan that pays that off as quickly as possible.

For anything with an interest rate higher than 15%, it's hard to imagine any expense not associated with your bare survival (food, shelter, gas) that should be prioritized above that. That includes really good things like contributing to your 401k; certainly, that includes things like going out to dinner, vacations, and streaming services.

For moderate interest rates between 8-15%, those should still be paid off quickly, although not with the urgency of the 15%+ debt. For those, it's probably okay to contribute to your 401k, but other expenses should be deprioritized until this debt is paid off.

No matter how you do it, you should have a plan on how you are going to do it.

2. Invest in a tax-advantaged account

Most people work at jobs that offer a 401k (or a 403b for non-profits). This is probably your most powerful tool to amass wealth. Its tax advantages are tremendous, and most companies offer a match which is a huge benefit. For those without access to one of these, an IRA acts in much the same way, albeit without the match and with lower annual contribution limits. Nonetheless, whether it's a 401k or an IRA, these accounts are powerful. You should be using them.

The math is profound. An average person (not a couple, just an individual mind you) could save 10% of their income into a 401k and 40 years later end up with $2.5 million ($40k starting salary, 3% wage increases up to $100k, 50% match, 10% stock returns). That's tremendous. Just that single, simple tool could get you to a level of financial freedom that very few today achieve.

When you start your job, set up your 401k. Set up a contribution level and then forget about it. Treat that deduction from your paycheck into your 401k just like you would payroll taxes, something that happens that you can't control so you don't think about it.

3. Get Asset Allocation right

As discussed before, Asset Allocation is probably the most important, least understood, and most commonly screwed up concept in personal finance. Make sure you get it right. You will always need to balance the need for higher returns (stocks) with the need for safety (bonds and cash). But remember that while stocks are much more volatile than bonds, that volatility decreases over longer time frames.

Where you have a very long-term time horizon you can enjoy the higher returns of stocks but with lower volatility just because you have years to ride out any rough patches in the stock market. Your 401k or IRA actually forces you to have a long-term time horizon. The money you put into those accounts in your 20s and 30s can't be touched for decades. You have years, and you should take advantage of that. It's hard to imagine a circumstance where a young person's 401k is invested in anything other than stocks, not cash or bonds or a balanced fund.

As you get older and closer to the time when you need that money, resist the urge to swing too far towards bonds and away from stocks. It is prudent to shift some, but don't overdo it. Remember that Vanguard recommends that someone in retirement have their portfolio at about 50% stocks, 50% bonds.

4. Invest in index mutual funds

Fees are important and they are riddled throughout the financial services industry. For most investors, the most common fees with be for investor advising and mutual fund management fees. After reading this book, you should be well-equipped to make most of your investment decisions without an advisor. As just mentioned, the primary savings tool for most should be a 401k and there's no reason you can't do that on your own. As your situation evolves and you amass more wealth and it requires more complexity an advisor may be appropriate, but certainly early on you can do it on your own.

Excessive mutual fund management fees are pervasive, and if you aren't paying attention, you will pay them without even knowing it. The simplest thing to do is exclusively invest in index mutual funds. When selecting your investments for your 401k or IRA, make sure the word "Index" is in the title. Bonus points if you look up the management fee (0.10% is a fair level as of the writing of this book), but you don't even need to do that. Just look for the word "index" and that will get you most of the way there.

If you're investing in a 401k they will have a limited list of funds you can choose from, so pick the index funds that are appropriate. If you are investing in an IRA you have many more choices. At Vanguard I would suggest VTSAX (US stocks) and VTIAX (international stocks); at Fidelity I would suggest FZROX (US stocks) and FZILX (international stocks).

5. Don't necessarily buy a home

Shelter expenses tend to be the single biggest line-item on a family's budget, so it's important to get this right. Homeownership is a complex and nuanced issue. There are plenty of reasons why buying a home makes a lot of sense, while there are others in favor of renting. That said, the loudest voices in our society consistently promote homeownership over renting as the universal solution for everyone. Resist the urge, and only buy a home if that's the right thing for you and your situation.

Owning has a lot of advantages—homes tend to increase in value, it builds equity, you have control of your life in a way you don't have with renting. Yet for a lot of those, the benefits aren't quite as good as they seem. Houses do increase in value over time, but less than most people think. Academic research has put the average annual home appreciation at 0.5%. Owning also allow you to build equity but you could easily take that extra money and invest it in stocks, likely getting a higher return.

Owning has a lot of disadvantages, although they are not commonly discussed—higher expenses, less flexibility. Property taxes, homeowner's insurance, association dues, and upkeep are all expenses a homeowner would have that a renter wouldn't (although those expenses are rolled into the rent); these can be significant. Another huge expense is associated with moving. Selling a home and buying a new one is a tremendously costly endeavor if you want to move. Somewhat associated with that is the lack of flexibility if you do want to move, be it across town or across the country. As a renter you can do so very easily and inexpensively, but that isn't the case as a homeowner.

There are pluses and minuses to both, so think about it as it applies best to your situation. If you're likely to be moving because of a job or a growing family, renting is likely the better option until you settle down.

Made in the USA
Columbia, SC
20 October 2024

44753110R00050